Organizational
Behavior

**Prentice-Hall International Series in
Industrial Engineering and Management Science**

W. Grant Ireson, *editor*

PRENTICE-HALL, INC.
PRENTICE-HALL INTERNATIONAL, INC., UNITED KINGDOM AND EIRE
PRENTICE-HALL OF CANADA, LTD., CANADA

Organizational
Behavior

PHILIP B. APPLEWHITE
Yale University

Prentice-Hall, Inc., Englewood Cliffs, New Jersey

PRENTICE-HALL INTERNATIONAL, INC., *London*
PRENTICE-HALL OF AUSTRALIA, PTY., LTD., *Sydney*
PRENTICE-HALL OF CANADA, LTD., *Toronto*
PRENTICE-HALL OF INDIA (PRIVATE) LTD., *New Delhi*
PRENTICE-HALL OF JAPAN, INC., *Tokyo*

Library of Congress Catalog Card Number 65-21799
Printed in the United States of America
C-64103

To Donald E. Porter
for his encouragement
with this book

Preface

This book is based on a review of the literature in organizational behavior. It presents no new theories, but rather attempts to integrate into a more meaningful whole the major research findings in this field. Copious use of quotes and reference citations has been made to preserve the flavor of the original research and to eliminate possible misinterpretations. Each chapter is somewhat independent of the others so that one area can be consulted at a time; however, the interrelationships of the chapters should be apparent. Whatever this book is, it is not a general theory of organizational behavior. Such a theory, documented by research findings, is needed and would advance the field considerably; the information presented here could be the minimum on which to base just such a theory.

I have adopted a specific concise approach to organizational behavior rather than an introductory one. Research findings are presented with only sufficient interpretation to make the authors' meanings clear. Occasionally, my interpretations of their findings and implications may be at variance with those of the original authors; I hope mine are the more conservative. The book is intended as a substitute for reviewing the vast literature of organizational behavior; of course, there is no real substitute for the original papers except a systems theory to inter-relate them.

I wish to thank the following for permission to quote: the Survey Research Center at the University of Michigan for *Satisfactions in the White Collar Job* by Nancy C. Morse, 1953 and *Productivity, Supervision, and Morale in an Office Situation* by Daniel Katz, Nathan Maccoby, and Nancy Morse, 1950; Harper and Row, Publishers for *Group Dynamics* by Dorwin Cartwright and Alvin Zander, 1960; Chandler Publishing Company for *Formal Organizations: A Comparative Study* by Peter M. Blau and W. Richard Scott, 1961; The Free Press of Glencoe (The Mac-millan Company) for *Handbook of Small Group Research* by A. Paul Hare, 1962; Addison-Wesley Publishing Company, Inc. for "Leadership" by Cecil A. Gibb in *Handbook of Social Psychology* edited by Gardner Lindzey, 1954.

P. B. A.

Contents

1 Introduction

Organizational behavior is the study of the ways in which individuals and groups behave in organizations—all kinds of organizations. If an organization is defined as two or more people, specialized in the functions each performs, working together toward some common goal, and governed by formal rules of behavior, then organizational behavior as an area of study is quite broad. It could encompass behavior in the family, in educational institutions, in military, government, business and industrial groups, to name a few. In studying behavior in this diverse class of organizations the unit of analysis is either the individual or groups of individuals or both; it is between the level of the individual qua physical being and the level of the encompassing organizational structure. If the organization as a whole were used, the area of study would be organizational theory and the concern would be with how the organization per se "behaves," develops, and is maintained. Organizational behavior, then, deals only with that behavior that in some way affects the operation of the organization or that develops as a result of organizational structure. The emphasis is upon the behavior of people either as individuals or in small groups, and not upon the behavior of the organization *in toto*.

Since organizational behavior deals with so many types of groups, it implies that there is something common to all the groups; that is, that there is a body of principles that applies to all groups. Indeed, if this were not the case, organizational behavior as a discipline would not exist; it would be a collection of unrelated facts, and results would be strictly limited to the group studied. At the present time, the assumption is that groups do possess similarities in the behavioral dimension such that research done with one group will yield results similar to the same research done with another group. This assumption cannot be proved in the absolute sense until studies of a particular aspect of behavior are carried out in many types of groups. In fact, it may well be better at this stage of behavioral science to concentrate efforts upon replicating experiments with many different types of groups to determine whether behavioral science findings are universal. So far the assumption of universality of findings has *generally* held. Therefore, if this be the case, then findings from industrial groups, say, should apply to military groups as well, and findings from laboratory groups should apply to "real" on-going groups.

Organizational behavior has as its goal the establishment of principles that explain and predict behavior statistically. Because Man does have free will he can always decide not to conform to whatever laws or principles behavioral scientists come up with. Because of this free will, behavioral scientists can only predict what most people will tend to do given a certain situation; they cannot predict what any given person will do. It is not possible to state in an absolute, non-probabilistic sense what any given person will do in any specific situation, for that person exerting his free will and knowing the behavioral predictions may simply decide not to act according to them. Probabilities have to be attached to behavioral science predictions. Perhaps, as the behavioral sciences and molecular biology merge it will be possible to state at a chemical level with *more* precision, why people behave as they do and when they will exhibit a specific behavior. The behavioral sciences are attempting to gather information about behavior, and there are certain rules that must be followed. The rules are those of science: observe, hypothesize, test the hypothesis, modify the original hypothesis, theorize. Where possible, the objective is to quantify the results. Intuition is important in designing research studies and interpreting results but it is no substitute for an actual study. One study, standing alone, does not prove anything in the behavioral sciences; rather, as implied, several similar studies are needed before a behavioral trend can be established. By this reasoning, nothing is ever "proved," as the word is used in the physical sciences, since it has yet to be shown that any kind of group is identical with any other kind of group.

It is not too infrequently stated by members of organizations that results in behavioral science, specifically those in organizational behavior, do not agree with their observations of the real world. Perhaps the research studies of organizational behavior are limited and do not apply to all situations; perhaps the people who object do not really understand the behavior around them and fail to perceive the true state of affairs. It is likely that both these reasons explain the discrepancy that sometimes exists between the findings of behavioral science and those of organizational managers. Since behavioral science seeks to understand and predict behavior, it has been accused, with a good deal of apprehension, of trying to manipulate it. There is no doubt that such organizations as unions, political groups, families, industrial organizations—to name a few—attempt to modify behavior, and their ability to do this may come from their use of behavioral science findings. But the behavioral sciences are relatively new to the world and attempts to manipulate behavior have been going on for millennia. Behavioral scientists are interested in how people behave, and when one begins to manipulate behavior he is not acting as a behavioral scientist, he is acting in another capacity. The physicist who develops the atomic bomb does not drop it on a country; if he were to do that he would not be acting as a physicist. This is not to say a scientist is not responsible for his discoveries. He is responsible as an individual in society but his is not the sole authority or power to restrict their use.

The purpose of this book is to gather together from diverse research studies the major findings of organizational behavior. The presentation is meant to be concise to avoid confusing research findings with subjective opinions and intuition. Practical applications of the findings are usually not explicitly stated but should follow fairly easily. The references at the end of this chapter are general and each one applies to most of the relevant topics in the discipline. The book by Kaplan (21) should be consulted for a philosophical appraisal of the methodology used in the behavioral sciences, and should be followed by a reading of *Research Methods in Social Relations* (24) which presents some of the actual methodology used.

In summary, it can be said that leaders and supervisors (Chapters 6, 7) make decisions (Chapter 4) which must be communicated (Chapter 5) to others; attitudes (Chapter 2) and group standards (Chapter 3) are affected and then serve to reaffect leaders and supervisors.

Introduction References

Papers

1. Leavitt, Harold J. and Bass, Bernard M. Organizational psychology. *Annual Review of Psychology* 1964, 15, 371–398.

2. Strodtbeck, Fred L. and Hare, A. Paul. Bibliography of small group research (1900–1953). *Sociometry* 1954, 17, 107–178.

3. Vroom, Victor H. and Maier, Norman R. F. Industrial social psychology. *Annual Review of Psychology* 1961, 12, 413–446.

Readings

4. Cartwright, Dorwin and Zander, Alvin. *Group Dynamics.* Evanston, Ill.: Row, Peterson & Company, 1960.

5. Costello, Timothy W. and Zalkind, Sheldon S. *Psychology in Administration.* Englewood Cliffs, New Jersey: Prentice-Hall, Inc., 1963.

6. Dubin, Robert. *Human Relations in Administration.* Englewood Cliffs, New Jersey: Prentice-Hall, Inc., 1961.

7. Etzioni, Amitai. *Complex Organizations.* New York: Holt, Rinehart & Winston, Inc., 1961.

8. Haire, Mason. *Modern Organization Theory.* New York: John Wiley & Sons, Inc., 1959.

9. Hare, A. Paul; Borgatta, Edgar F. and Bales, Robert F. *Small Groups.* New York: Alfred A. Knopf, Inc., 1955.

10. Leavitt, Harold J. *The Social Science of Organizations.* Englewood Cliffs, New Jersey: Prenctice-Hall, Inc., 1963.

11. Litterer, Joseph A. *Organizations: Structure and Behavior.* New York: John Wiley & Sons, Inc., 1963.

12. Mailick, Sidney and Van Ness, Edward H. *Concepts and Issues in Administrative Behavior.* Englewood Cliffs, New Jersey: Prentice-Hall, Inc., 1962.

13. Porter, Donald E. and Applewhite, Philip B. *Studies in Organizational Behavior and Management.* Scranton, Pennsylvania: International Textbook Company, 1964.

14. Rubenstein, Albert H. and Haberstroh, Chadwick J. *Some Theories of Organization.* Homewood, Illinois: Richard D. Irwin, Inc., 1960.

15. Sutermeister, Robert A. *People and Productivity.* New York: McGraw-Hill Book Company, 1963.

Texts

16. Blau, Peter M. and Scott, W. Richard. *Formal Organizations.* San Francisco: Chandler Publishing Co., 1962.

17. Bonner, Hubert. *Group Dynamics.* New York: The Ronald Press Company, 1959.

18. Dubin, Robert. *The World of Work.* Englewood Cliffs, New Jersey: Prentice-Hall, Inc., 1958.

19. Hare, A. Paul. *Handbook of Small Group Research.* New York: Free Press of Glencoe, Inc., 1962.

20. Homans, George C. *Social Behavior: Its Elementary Forms.* New York: Harcourt, Brace and World, Inc., 1961.

21. Kaplan, Abraham. *The Conduct of Inquiry.* San Francisco: Chandler Publishing Co., 1964.

22. March, James G. and Simon, Herbert A. *Organizations.* New York: John Wiley & Sons, Inc., 1958.

23. Pfiffner, John M. and Sherwood, Frank P. *Administrative Organization.* Englewood Cliffs, New Jersey: Prentice-Hall, Inc., 1960.

24. Seltiz, Claire; Jahoda, Marie; Deutsch, Morton and Cook, Stuart W. *Research Methods in Social Relations.* New York: Holt, Rinehart & Winston, Inc., 1959.

25. Simon, Herbert A. *Administrative Behavior.* New York: The Macmillan Company, 1957.

26. Thibaut, John W. and Kelley, Harold H. *The Social Psychology of Groups.* New York: John Wiley & Sons, Inc., 1959.

27. Thompson, Victor A. *Modern Organization.* New York: Alfred A. Knopf, Inc., 1961.

2 Job Satisfaction and Morale: Attitudes and Motivation

At one time or another, almost everyone has ascribed the words "morale" or "satisfaction" to themselves or others to indicate feelings of contentment. And, comments to the effect that satisfied workers produce more than unhappy ones have been quite common. Morale, job satisfaction, contentment, and "worker happiness" mean all things to all people. In an industrial environment, these words are seldom defined and dealt with consistently. It appears "logical" that people who are satisfied more will produce more simply because this is human nature—but is it?

The problem, if any is ascertained at this level, appears quite academic, a matter of semantics. But actually the problem is not just one of terminology; it involves feelings and emotions. "Job satisfaction" and "morale" are the words most frequently used in referring to how people doing all types of work feel and think about their jobs. It may be that employees actually regard job satisfaction as the only dimension, other than monetary, by which to judge a job. At first thought, the physical environment, that is, the

6

noise, illumination, temperature, safety, etc., would seem to be the prime determinant of how well a worker liked his job. The immediate physical surroundings, if they meet some minimal criteria that guarantee physical comfort, hardly seem critical, though. Further thought may consider the work group and the social interactions evolving from them as related to morale and job satisfaction. A man may dislike the actual physical work but enjoy the people with whom he is working and, therefore, have a satisfying job. Then, too, a person's attitude towards his work is colored by experiences of boredom, fatigue and monotony. What of his wages? Does not this lead to satisfaction in some way? Given a certain monetary income, almost any job can be tolerable and hence, perhaps, satisfying. A general economic slump, a state of industrial labor unrest, or a company's inconsistent employee relations policies can be fear- or anxiety-producing factors that affect the emotions and produce attitudes about the job relevant to satisfaction and the worker's morale.

It should be apparent now that the factors relating to job satisfaction and morale are quite numerous and complicated, ranging from physical working conditions through the social environment surrounding the job to external economic factors. But all of this is a subjective approach to listing the components of morale and satisfaction. The only way to see what the components are is to enter an industrial or office setting and ferret out, by social research methods, the relevant dimensions. As a first approximation to these components, the studies (60, 61, 62) by Walker point up some interesting findings.

The "man on the assembly line" did not feel that job content (what is actually done on the job) was the main source of satisfaction but rather, that satisfaction was a sum-total measure of the people met, the opportunities, the prestige, and the money and security of the job. This same group of workers responding to what they thought influenced job satisfaction reported good hours, nearness to work, and good working conditions as being relevant. But Walker and Guest conclude, "good working conditions, however desirable, don't make the job good" (61, p. 105), that is, satisfying. "Job happiness," then, enters the picture and is said to be a function of the worker's control over the assembly lines. Generally, the more rush and repetition on the assembly line, the less the job satisfaction of the men.

The workers Walker and Guest interviewed said also "that a good foreman (or at least one who got along with the men) was an element in the degree of job satisfaction" (61, p. 96). Furthermore, a "close relation to the product . . . is often a positive factor in producing personal satisfaction" (60, p. 200). A summary of the author's findings would indicate that almost everything was related to job satisfaction— and it may well be. When the workers speak of their job likes, they speak of happy, satisfying jobs and mention many factors as being relevant. These studies indicate that the following variables were mentioned as being related to job satisfaction: (1) salary, (2) security, (3) prestige, (4) job uncertainty, (5) working conditions, (6) physical distance from work, (7) psychological distance from the product produced, (8) number of years on the job, (9) number of friends on the job, (10) absenteeism, (11) ratings by immediate superiors, and (12) desirability of living in the area around the plant. That job satisfaction is a complex of attitudes is evident.

It is interesting to note that the worker (61) spoke of personal job attitudes, the foreman (62), of group job attitudes. Foremen talk of group tensions, feelings, morale and of organization and team relationships rather than of individual feelings. Not that the foremen made an explicit distinction between morale and job satisfaction, but at least group satisfactions were set aside from individual job satisfactions. This hints at the fact that job satisfaction is an individual thing while morale is a group concept.

These studies by Walker *et al.* as part of the Yale Technology Project were not specifically designed to measure job satisfaction and morale and for this reason, cannot be criticized on this account. They are case studies, limited in scope not only to a specific industrial type of plant but also in the refinement of research techniques used. The studies are valuable in indicating the general flavor of assembly line work and particularly in evolving some ideas about job satisfaction and morale. Because of the informality in eliciting the attitudes of the workers, it is probable that differently worded questions would produce different responses because attitudes cannot often be measured directly, because of a reluctance to answer direct questions. A quick and relatively simple look at job satisfaction and morale has been presented—probably typical of most of the feelings of factory workers in industry. However, a more rigorous and limited look at job satisfaction and morale is necessary before an accurate understanding of these concepts is attained. Since a sophisticated approach to these concepts will be undertaken, the separation of job satisfaction and morale will be made now, based initially on the previous comments made by the workers in Walker's studies. Actually, where both morale and job satisfaction are dealt with in a single study, some authors (14, 15, 17, 21, 23, 32, 33, 36, 64) make no distinction between the two, while other authors (1, 2, 3, 6, 16, 25, 49, 52, 65) do. There really is no conflict between those who do and those who do not separate satisfaction and morale, because those who do not never present any argument why satisfaction and morale should mean the same thing. In other words, they implicitly assume there is no difference. As the chapter develops, research findings will be presented that indicate the necessity of separating of these two variables, at least on a conceptual level.

Job Satisfaction

A good introduction to this notion of job satisfaction can be gained by considering in some detail some of the early attempts to pin down job satisfaction as a well-defined concept and relate it to such things as productivity. Two rather good early attempts along this line were *Productivity, Supervision, and Morale in an Office Situation* by Katz, Maccoby, and Morse (23) written in 1950 and *Satisfactions in the White Collar Job* by Morse (33) in 1953. The study by Katz, Maccoby, and Morse will be considered in some detail to give some insight about the way in which the research results were obtained.

Their research was carried on in the Prudential Insurance Company, a company employing 10,000 people at the home office. From this population, 419 non-supervisory employees and 24 section heads or supervisors were selected in such a way that there were 12 high productivity and 12 low productivity groups with their section heads. The groups were matched to form 12 high-low productivity pairs; each pair did the the same type of work (parallel operations), had the same aptitude scores on tests, the same distribution of wages, age, length of service, lived about the same distance away from work, and had the same satisfaction with their housing and community. This matching enabled comparisons to be made between high and low productivity groups with all variables except productivity and satisfaction held constant. Since the 12 paired groups covered work ranging from "highly routine typing to skilled calculation" in the servicing of insurance policies, job satisfaction and productivity could be measured over a wide range of activities. It is interesting to note that the differences in productivity between the high and low production groups was seldom more than 10% (p. 10).

The size of each group varied from about 6 to 32 people. Of the non-supervisory employees, 82% were women while in the supervisory group, 63% were women. Of the employees, 76% were high school graduates or better; of the supervisors, 63% were high school graduates or better. With regard to age distribution for the employees, 46% were between 17 and 24, 44% between 25 and 44; for the supervisors, 50% were between 35 and 40 and 46% were older than 40. With regard to length of service with the company, for the employees: 26% were with the company 2 years or less, 11% between 2 and 5 years, 37% between 5 and 20 years, 25% more than 20 years; for supervisors: 4% less than 15 years, 21% between 15 and 20 years, 58% between 21 and 25 years, and 17% greater than 25 years. This information must be considered before generalizing the results of this study.

A group of questions to present, in different forms, to the employees and supervisors was drawn up and given orally. The interviewer would copy the worker's responses to specific questions asked; replies were in the form of "free answers" that had to be coded into some standardized form for analysis. Particular emphasis was placed on the employees' attitudes toward questions about (1) their work group, (2) their job, (3) company policies, (4) job status and salary, and (5) supervision. The interview length was approximately one and one-half hours per employee.

Seven categories composed the questions given the supervisors. Here are some examples of questions asked under each of the category headings (pp. 68-74):

A. *Job Content:* (1) "What do you do in your job?" (2) "How well do you like this sort of work?"

B. *Job Aspirations:* (1) "What were your plans and ambitions before you started working?" (2) "What are your plans and ambitions now?"

C. *Attitudes toward Company* (1) "How do you like working for Prudential?"

D. *Relationships with Staff:* (1) "To whom do you usually go for advice in matters concerning your work?" (2) "What kind of group spirit or morale is there in your section?"

E. *Employee's Evaluation of His Job and Section:* (1) How would you like to see training of people in your section handled?" (2) "Do the people in your section get a feeling of accomplishment from the work they are doing?"

F. *Attitude toward Company Policies and Practices:* (1) "How do you feel about the way things are done in the department?" (2) "How well satisfied are you with your present salary?"

G. *General Attitudes:* (1) "What are the main gripes or dissatisfactions of employees here at Prudential?" (2) "Suppose a friend of yours came to work for Prudential, what advice would you give him?"

The interview length per supervisor was about two and one-half hours.

It was decided to have four measures of something called essentially general job satisfaction (contrary to the title of this study, satisfaction, and *not* morale, is being dealt with). These four measures are: (1) *pride in work group*—"satisfaction with the accomplishment of the immediate or secondary work group of which the employee is a member" (p. 39); (2) *intrinsic job satisfaction*—"satisfaction obtained by the individual employee from performing those tasks which constitute the content of

Job satisfaction Component

his job" (p. 42); (3) *company involvement*—the "degree to which the employee derives satisfaction from and identifies with the company in which he is employed" (p. 43); and (4) *financial and job status satisfaction*—"satisfaction the employee has with his present and expected earnings and with the status of his present and expected position in the company" (p. 44). Groups of questions in the interview covered each of these attitude measures, and the coding of the answers formed the basis of the values of these measures.

The results of the analysis showed that *pride in work group* was the only measure of job satisfaction "which shows a distinct relationship to productivity" (p. 48); that is, the high production groups showed greater pride in their work group than did the low production group. However, the cause-effect relationship is not quite clear in that the high production group may have more pride (i.e., be satisfied) because they know they are high producers rather than being high producers because they are satisfied. Furthermore, the study showed that "the section heads of the low productivity sections supervise their employees more closely than do the section heads of the high producing groups" (p. 17). Then, it is possible to say the high productivity groups were more satisfied with their production accomplishments because their section heads did not prod them into it. On the other hand, since some groups were high producers, their section heads did not have to prod them. The point is again the ambiguity of the cause-effect relationship.

The authors suggested that the measure *intrinsic job satisfaction* did not relate to production fluctuations because neither factor varied "sufficiently in this study to permit a relationship, if one really existed, to be found" (p. 52). As mentioned before, the difference between the high and low productivity groups was seldom more than 10%. It was also suggested that intrinsic job satisfaction and productivity were related only at the extremes of their ranges and not in the middle! "Thus there may be a positive correlation between intrinsic job satisfaction and productivity when productivity is very high or low but not when productivity and job satisfaction are both somewhere in the middle of their ranges" (p. 52). It was suggested that further research be done to see how intrinsic job satisfaction is affected by the level of aspiration; it is apparent that workers who have aspirations higher than existing opportunities will become dissatisfied (p. 53).

Figures were previously given concerning age distribution, length of service, etc. All these were mentioned because, while they are controlled variables in the study, they are important in transferring the results of the study to another situation. These variables are age, sex, size of work group, type of work, education, type of supervision, and length of service with the company. It is not quite accurate to apply the results of this study to another situation where there is a significant difference between the two sets of variables. Other studies employing these and other variables for other types of jobs must be looked at to gain a better idea of the "univerals" of job satisfaction.

A study done by Morse (33) in a similar office situation approximated the same cross section as that of the previous study; that is, 84% of the 742 employees studied were women, 79% high school graduates or better, 53% less than 25 years old, etc. Morse is aware that this does not constitute a random sample of this country's employee population and states that "the results on employee satisfaction should be interpreted with full realization of the particular characteristics of this population" (p. 7) and that "many of the findings may not hold true for blue-collar employees" (p. 10).

An interview schedule was devised to measure general employee satisfaction by the same four components (intrinsic job satisfaction, company involvement, financial and job status satisfaction, and pride-in-group performance) as were used in the study *Productivity, Supervision and Morale in an Office Situation*. As before, these components were arranged from the scoring of the employees' responses to questions asked in the interviews. Intercorrelations between these four measures were less than .44, with pride-in-group performance having essentially a zero correlation with the other three measures; this indicates that each of these components is significantly different. It should be noted that, by definition, these four components are assumed to be measures of general employee satisfaction —in no way has it been "proved" that this is the case. The results are, then, a function of the questions asked.

As in the previous study, Morse found that "those groups who were more satisfied with their jobs, the company and with their pay and job status were not necessarily those which were most productive" (p. 115). Before some of the other interesting results of the study are interpreted, its limitations (p. 11) should be mentioned. In the interview, the employees were asked both about their satisfaction and about working conditions, but it is possible that the employees' degree of satisfaction affected their perception of working conditions. Causal relations in this study must also be inferred, since there was no experimental manipulation of variables to determine which phenomenon is cause and which effect. The sampling errors have already been discussed.

But despite these limitations, the theoretical discussion of job satisfaction that Morse develops is worth considering. Tension level is equated with the needs of individuals in that the higher the tension level, the stronger that person's needs. Certain physical and social elements in the environment can reduce the tension level by meeting his needs. Anything that reduces this tension level can be considered as satisfying. "The

amount of satisfaction experienced by the individual is a function of:
(1) how much his needs are fulfilled by being in a particular situation
. . . and (2) how much his needs remain unfulfilled" (p. 32). When the
tension level is lowered, that is, when the needs are being met, satisfaction
will result. The satisfaction an employee experiences appears "to be a
function of both what he wanted from a situation and what he obtained
from it" (p. 27). Essentially, then, "a worker who aspires to little may
be entirely happy with a very modest job . . . a worker whose aspiration
level continues to rise as his own achievements rise may never feel that
his company has properly recognized his abilities" (p. 75).

Morse's approach is by no means unique; rather it is the "standard"
way of approaching satisfaction. Schaffer has used the term "dissatisfaction" to mean "a conscious recognition of a state of tension" (47,
p. 2). Where Morse would say "the most productive workers are the ones
who have the strongest needs for which productivity is a path" (33,
p. 127), Schaffer would say "over-all job satisfaction will vary directly
with the extent to which those needs of an individual which can be satisfied in a job are actually satisfied" (47, p. 3)—which means, if the needs
are productivity, then those workers with this need will be high producers.
Schaffer and Morse agree on this point and so do many other researchers.
Gordon defines high satisfaction "as the feeling of well-being experienced
by an individual when his needs are being filled to his satisfaction" (14,
p. 3). Herzberg, Mausner, and Snyderman state that when at least some
"satisfying" factors of the job in general are present in a worker's specific
job, "the fulfillment of his basic needs is such that he enters a period of
exceptional positive feelings about his job" (18, p. 69).

Spector (49) has proposed frustration, gratification, and expectation
hypotheses that summarize quite well the notion of aspirations and expectations vis-á-vis satisfaction. His frustration hypothesis says, "on failing to
achieve an attractive goal, an individual's [satisfaction] will be higher if the
probability of achieving that goal had been perceived to be low than if it
had been perceived to be high" (p. 52). Failure to reach a goal given a
low expectation of reaching it will result in less dissatisfaction than if
there were high expectations of reaching the goal. The converse of the
frustration hypothesis is the gratification hypothesis: "on achieving an
attractive goal, an individual's [satisfaction] will be higher if the probability
of achieving that goal had been perceived to be low than if it had been
perceived to be high" (p. 52). If a person has low expectations about
reaching a goal, then if he reaches the goal he will be more satisfied than
if he had higher expectations about reaching it. According to these two
hypotheses, the greater the disparity between expectation and achievement
with achievement being the higher, the greater the satisfaction. His expectation hypothesis says "on succeeding, or failing, to achieve an attractive

goal, an individual's [satisfaction] will be higher if the probability of achieving that goal had been perceived to be low than if it had been perceived to be high" (p. 52). This hypothesis is merely a summary of the other two, and the other two follow from it.

Vroom (59) introduces the notion of ego-satisfaction into the general framework of job satisfaction. A person is ego-involved in his job "to whatever extent his self-esteem is affected by his perceived level of performance" (p. 161), where ego-involvement means getting oneself personally involved. In studying 489 blue collar workers in a Canadian refinery, he found that "the satisfaction of persons who are ego-involved in their jobs is more affected by the extent to which their jobs give them an opportunity for self-expression" (p. 175) than by other factors. By this token, job satisfaction for job ego-involved workers will result from self-expression in their jobs. A hypothesis for this might be: "the more ego-involved a person is in his job the greater the positive relationship between the amount of his opportunity for self-expression in that job and his job satisfaction" (p. 163). At first thought, this hypothesis leaves no room for the notion of expectations, and for ego-involved people this may be of no consequence. However, the amount of actual self-expression compared to that expected may produce different degrees of satisfaction, and the expectation-aspiration notions will still hold. It seems that this desire for self-expression fulfills a need and results in satisfaction. Using a laboratory situation involving 44 college students, Trow (55) found that the need of autonomy when met would produce job satisfaction. He defines autonomy as "the degree to which a person's position in the information flow of an organization permits him to determine for himself the organizationally appropriate level or direction of his own future activity" (p. 204). Although autonomy is not exactly the same as self-expression, it is sufficiently similar to say that it measures the same thing. Then Trow's finding in the laboratory that "the job satisfaction of a person in a task-oriented group is determined to a large extent by . . . the autonomy of the position he occupies in the information flow, greater autonomy producing higher satisfaction" (p. 208) is equivalent to Vroom's finding in the refinery. The studies both indicate that the worker's doing what he wants to do contributes to the satisfaction of a major need, but it is a major need only when he is ego-involved (Vroom) and/or his other dimensions of satisfaction are limited (Trow). In Trow's study, the situation is artificial—these are students taking part in an experiment, not people working for a living, subject to the desires and needs of the full-time working man. Studies actually done in industry (18, 35, 47) have shown that this need for autonomy or self-expression is *not* necessarily the most important need.

The two approaches to satisfaction that have been developed pertain to expectations (aspirations) and needs. Needs themselves can exist in the form of expectations, since a person attaches some expectation to satisfying his needs. This phenomenon is not necessarily explicit—it occurs because meeting the expectations of needs does cause satisfaction. Needs are the key to understanding satisfaction; thus it becomes necessary to state what the more important needs are and what criteria they follow. Schaffer (47, p. 4) lists six criteria which a list of important needs should conform to. They should be: (1) "a rather permanent and stable part of . . . personality structure" so that a basic set of needs once determined will suffice for further studies; (2) "relatively important in the determination of adjustment"—the needs should be over-all related to "personality" adjustments to industrial life; (3) "present in many people" in order to approach the problem on a more nearly universal basis; (4) "conceivably . . . satisfied in a work environment" so that they relate to job satisfaction rather than to satisfactions primarily outside the job; (5) "definable and unique"—ready to be used operationally, with little overlap between needs; (6) "amenable to measurement by a paper-and-pencil questionnaire" which is easier and cheaper than, say, depth interviewing. Schaffer (47, pp. 4–5) lists 12 needs that he feels meet the above criteria. Herzberg, Mausner, and Snyderman (18, p. 44) list 14 needs which are elements "in which the respondent finds a source for his good or bad feelings about the job."

Schaffer conducted his study with 72 professional and semi-professional men in four different organizations (an industrial manufacturing plant, a department store, a government agency, and a vocational guidance agency) —a sample "obviously atypical of the total working force," to use Schaffer's own comments. He established, on the basis of questionnaire results, an average need hierarchy for the sample used. What he had, therefore, was a rank ordering from most important to least important of the 12 needs he proposed. Herzberg, *et al.,* conducted their study with 200 employees (engineers and accountants) in nine different companies (four industrial plants, a utility company, and four office staffs), and he also obtained a rank ordering of those needs which contributed (from the most to the least) toward favorable job attitudes. A similar study by Myers (35) conducted at Texas Instruments, Inc. involved 230 men and 52 women in five groups: scientists, engineers, manufacturing supervisors, technicians (paid by the hour), and women assemblers (paid by the hour). By the interview technique, a rank ordering of the most important needs for each group was obtained. Table 1 presents a comparison of these three studies by Schaffer, by Herzberg, *et al.,* and by Myers.

Absolutely speaking, there are, of course, differences among the needs listed for each group although responsibility is near the top of most of them. It is not surprising that these needs apply very definitely to the work situation as part of the total life situation, where man, per se, perhaps has

Table 1. Employee Needs (Rank Ordered)

SCHAFFER	HERZBERG, et al.	MYERS					
PROFESSIONAL MEN	ENGINEERS AND ACCOUNTANTS	ENGINEERS	SCIENTISTS	MANUFACTURING SUPERVISORS	TECHNICIANS	FEMALE ASSEMBLERS	
1. Creativity and challenge	Achievement +	Work itself +	Responsibility −	Advancement +	Responsibility +	Competence of supervision	1.
2. Achievement	Recognition +	Responsibility −	Work itself +	Responsibility	Advancement +	Recognition −	2.
3. Social welfare ("need to help others")	Work itself +	Company policy and administration −	Company policy and administration +	Pay −	Pay −	Security −	3.
4. Moral value scheme (need to have behavior agree with this scheme)	Responsibility +	Pay −	Recognition +	Achievement +	Work itself −	Friendliness of supervision +	4.
5. Interpersonal relationships	Advancement +	Advancement +	Competence of supervision	Possibility of growth +	Company policy and administration +	Pay +	5.
6. Self-expression	Salary −	Recognition −	Advancement +	Friendliness of supervision −	Achievement	Achievement +	6.
7. Dominance	Possibility of growth	Achievement	Achievement	Company policy and administration	Competence of supervision −	Work itself −	7.

16

No.	Factor	Factor	Sign
8.	Recognition	Interpersonal relations (subordinates)	
9.	Economic security	Status	−
10.	Independence	Interpersonal relations (superior)	−
11.	Socio-economic status	Interpersonal relations (peers)	
12.	Dependence	Supervision-technical	−
13.		Company policy and administration	−
14.		Working conditions	−
15.		Factors in personal life	
16.		Job security	

Right-hand column (rank 9.–16.):

- ⎰ Competence of supervision / Friendliness of supervision ⎱ −
- Recognition +
- ⎰ Competence of supervision / Peer relations ⎱
- Recognition
- ⎰ Company policy and administration / Peer relations ⎱ −

9.
10.
11.
12.
13.
14.
15.
16.

KEY: those in parentheses are nearly equal in rank; + lead to satisfaction (primarily); − lead to dissatisfaction (primarily); those unmarked are bipolar (primarily).

similar basic needs—as Maslow (29) would suggest. However, in a work situation differences in needs are to be expected because of differences in job aspirations (involving education, socio-economic status, etc.). A woman working on an assembly line has little concern with advancement, since this is not a reasonable expectation; however, a supervisor's main motivation or drive may be toward advancement. Further research of this same type will have to be done on different work groups before any firm conclusions on motivation are reached.

Schaffer correlated an over-all job satisfaction measure for each individual with the mean of the 12 need satisfaction scores for each individual and got a correlation coefficient of + .44. This is to say, knowing an individual's mean score on these needs, it is possible to predict his over-all satisfaction. When he correlated each individual's over-all job satisfaction score with the mean of the first and second highest need satisfaction scores for each individual, the correlation coefficient rose to + .58, increasing the accuracy of prediction.

Herzberg and his colleagues found, rather interestingly, that not all of their 16 needs or factors were bipolar with respect to job satisfaction; that is, they would contribute invariably either to satisfaction if met *or* dissatisfaction if not met. Rather, most of them were polar, contributing to satisfaction if the need were met *or* to dissatisfaction if the need were not met, but not neccessarily evoking the opposite reaction. The important point is that fulfilling a need that is polar with respect to the dissatisfaction side of the continuum will not cause the need to contribute significantly to satisfaction. Likewise, not fulfilling a need that is polar with respect to the satisfaction side of the continuum will not cause the need to contribute significantly to dissatisfaction. The contributors to *job satisfaction*, if met, were: achievement, recognition, work itself, responsibility, and advancement. These needs if not met did not cause dissatisfaction but rather went to some neutral point. The contributors to *job dissatisfaction* were: company policy and administration, supervision (technical), interpersonal relations (superior), and working conditions (p. 81). These needs if met did not cause satisfaction but, again, went to some neutral point, instead of increasing to the point where they began contributing to satisfaction. Myers' results are also indicated in Table 1.

Maslow (29) has proposed a hierarchy of human needs listed in order of importance, to account for the differential effects that certain "environmental returns" have. At the lowest level are the physiological needs (hunger, thirst, etc.); after these are satisfied to a certain unspecified extent, the next need in the hierarchy, safety, becomes important. Once the individual feels this need is sufficiently satisfied, he will look toward the next highest need, and so on through belongingness, esteem, self-actualization, and aesthetic needs. These needs are not mutually exclusive, nor is it claimed that everyone has the same specific ordering. It is useful in appraising, say, the value of an increasing-pay incentive system. Money will provide what is necessary to satisfy the more basic needs of hunger and safety from the elements, but after a point another form of environmental return is necessary. Interpersonal relationships provide a return that can satisfy the belongingness need—an increase in pay cannot, per se, satisfy this need. Hence no increase in pay will motivate the individual to work for psychological returns which are not forthcoming with monetary rewards. Necessities for life may be termed "needs," but needs relating to job satisfaction are "wants," relating only to the lesser sphere of the job and not to life.

Porter (38) has studied 64 first-level supervisors and 75 middle-level managers in three different companies to determine the extent to which their needs in a modified Maslow hierarchy have been met. They filled out questionnaires that attempted to determine the importance of and any deficiencies of five needs in a hierarchy. The needs, from the least important up, are security, social, esteem (prestige), autonomy (independence), and self-actualization (personal growth and development). It was hypothesized that "lower-level management positions were more likely to produce deficiencies in fulfillment of psychological needs than were middle-level positions" (p. 8), and an analysis of the questionnaires did indicate this. Presumably, both levels of management agree as to the relative importance of the needs, but lower-level management's duties are not challenging enough to satisfy the higher needs of esteem, autonomy, and self-actualization. In a larger study, Porter (39) found similar results. Of course, these needs could be broken down into job satisfaction wants.

If the important needs are lumped together to form a general need, then would not a general satisfaction suffice? Could this notion of job satisfaction be related or even be equivalent to something called "general satisfaction"? Brayfield, Wells, and Strate (8) did a study to answer this question. Using "41 male and 52 female city government office employees," they found that "job satisfaction and general satisfaction were positively and significantly related among the males; no significant relationships were obtained among the females" (p. 205). If a significant positive relationship was shown for *both* the male and female employees, it could be said that this was due to the fact that job satisfaction accounted for most of the general satisfaction for men and women. As a relationship only held for the men, the researches suggested that "when the job is perceived as important in the life scheme as may be the case for the males here, general satisfaction becomes a function, in part at least, of job satisfaction" (p. 205). For the men, the job is a major part of their life (accounting for about 24% of the week, with sleep accounting for 33% of the week leaving only 43% of the week "free"), and it seems reasonable that being satisfied on the job would account a great deal for being generally satisfied with life. For women this is not traditionally so. But since job satisfaction is a component of general satisfaction, it seems easier to measure job satisfaction itself, rather than "general satisfaction," from which job satisfaction would be deduced. The studies by Porter are concerned with the satisfaction of Maslow's needs and therefore relate to general satisfaction. (Needs in Maslow's sense are relevant to general satisfaction while specific job "wants" are related to job satisfaction.) If life's needs and job wants were the same, then general satisfaction would equal job satisfaction.

It has been shown that wants and aspirations form the basis of job satisfaction, but it is now necessary to indicate the operational groupings of wants as components of satisfaction. Several wants can be grouped together to form a dimension of job satisfaction; these dimensions (or elements) define job satisfaction. However, establishing a sufficient number

Table 2. Job Satisfaction Components

KATZ, MACCOBY AND MORSE (23); MORSE (33)	KAHN (20)	STAGNER, FLEBBE, AND WOOD (51)
1. Pride in work group		
2. Intrinsic job satisfaction		1. General working conditions
3. Company involvement	1. Organization worked for	2. Union-management relations
4. Financial and job status satisfaction	2. Wages, promotions, and mobility	
	3. Supervision	3. General quality of supervision
	4. Job prestige	
		4. Grievance handling procedures
Year of Study		
1950, 1953	1951	1952

of dimensions is *not* an intuitive process—it depends on factor analysis techniques. It will be recalled that Katz, Maccoby, and Morse (23) and Morse (33) listed four dimensions or components of general job satisfaction: Pride in work group, intrinsic job satisfaction, company involvement, and financial and job status satisfaction. Consider also what other researchers have found to measure general job satisfaction. Kahn (20) in working with foremen in a tractor factory found the components of job satisfaction to be attitudes toward: supervision, organization worked for, job prestige, wages and promotions and mobility (these three being a composite attitude). Stagner, Flebbe, and Wood (51) found the important job satisfaction factors for 715 male unionized railroad workers to be: union-management relations, grievance handling procedures, general quality of supervision, and general working conditions. Such results, the authors point out are not surprising in a heavily unionized industry. Gadel (13) found in studying 301 women (60% were at least 40 years old and most were married) doing typing and routine clerical work that

Gadel (13) Younger Employees	Gadel (13) Older Employees	Ross and Zander (46)	Sinha (48)
1. Co-workers			1. Work group
2. Working conditions	1. Hours worked	1. Autonomy 2. Doing important work	2. Type of work
	2. Company prestige		
3. Pay 4. Advancement	3. Security		
	4. Supervision	3. Fair evaluation of work	3. Supervisory behavior
			4. Job status
5. Ease of commuting to work			
		4. Recognition	
1953	1953	1957	1958

the important job satisfaction components for the younger group of women were type of work, working conditions, pay, co-workers, ease of commuting to work, and advancement opportunities. For the older employees, Gadel found security, supervision, company prestige, and hours of working essential. In studying skilled women in a large company, Ross and Zander (46) found the main components of general job satisfaction to be recognition, autonomy, doing important work, and fair evaluation of work done. Sinha (48) reports the following components in India: job status, type of work, supervisory behavior, and work group. Table 2 summarizes the above findings.

In preparing Table 2, the components from different studies that seemed alike were grouped together so that each row contains essentially similar components. The rows cannot be said to correlate exactly because certain of the components are subsets of others, i.e., Hours Worked is a subset of Working Conditions. The comparison, then, is primarily conceptual. It is seen that there is not complete agreement between columns, either; several explanations may be offered. *First,* the studies really are the same (measure the same thing), and the differences are purely semantic. *Second,* if the studies are the same, then sampling errors contribute, along with semantic differences to apparent differences. *Third,* real differences do obtain between the studies, and these are due to each study's sample requiring different components for shifting populations. *Fourth,* job satisfaction components may change over time both with respect to all workers (a moving average) and with respect to each worker. It is by no means clear at this time what the explanation is. Counting the entries across the rows and selecting the rows with the most entries, it could be stated that the main components of general job satisfaction are (1) attitude toward work group, (2) general working conditions, (3) attitude toward company, (4) monetary benefits, and (5) attitudes toward supervision. These are the "wants" workers seek to satisfy.

Morale

It was pointed out in the introduction that some authors make a distinction between morale and job satisfaction while others do not. Viteles has defined morale as a "willingness to strive for the goals of a particular group" (58, p. 12). Quite simply, "morale is a group phenomenon" (2, p. 73) and "must always be defined in terms of an individual-group relationship" (5, p. 125). The term morale should apply to groups and not to individuals except where the individual is directly related to the group. That is, an individual can be said to have high morale only when he is related to a group. It makes little sense to say a person has high morale when he stands alone, divorced from a group. The key, then, to morale is the group, which is defined as at least two persons working together toward some common goal. The notion of "togetherness" may be quite general and is tied up with a common goal. In a military situation the goal may be to destroy a gun emplacement; in an industrial organization, it may be a higher departmental efficiency rating; in a political party, it may be to win an election. "Morale is a condition of congruent motivation among members of a group resulting in relatively high levels of energy expenditure toward common goals" (25, p. 73). If there is sufficient motivation for the members of the group to put forth extra effort in the achievement of group goals, then high morale for this group exists (16). Morale is a measure of the summed motivations of group members to work together toward a common goal—this is "group" morale. "Individual" morale is just a measure of an individual's motivation to pursue with others the common goal of the group of which he is a member.

Blum has defined industrial morale "as the possession of a feeling . . . of being accepted by and belonging to a group of employees through adherence to common goals and confidence in the desirability of these goals" (5, p. 77). This definition approaches that of group cohesiveness, discussed in another chapter, simply defined as a measure of the group's attractiveness to individuals. If a group's goals are attractive to an individual then the individual will *tend* to have high morale with regard to the group, according to Blum's definition. But high morale will actually be present *only* when the individual works toward the group's common goal. Stagner defines morale "as an index of the extent to which the individual perceives a probability of satisfying his own motives through cooperation with the group" (52, p. 64). When the individuals' motives and goals are identical with the group's, morale will be at its maximum value. When a common goal for group and for individual develops, morale is present in the participation the individual has in the group. All of the above definitions are consistent with each other, but they do cover slightly different aspects of the concept of morale. However, when considering all the literature on morale, such unity is not prevalent.

Blum has listed some of the determinants of morale as "group cooperation, need for a goal, observable progress toward the goal, and specific tasks . . . which can move the group toward the goal" (5, p. 183). While these may determine morale, they cannot be thought of as operationally defining it. On the other hand, Roach (43) did a study of 2,072 clerical and management employees by administering an employee opinion survey and obtained rather specific determinants of morale. A factor analysis of the morale components revealed 12 factors (pp. 421–430): (1) general attitude toward company, (2) general attitude toward supervision, (3) satisfaction with job standards, (4) the consideration the supervisor shows worker, (5) work load and work pressure, (6) degree of treatment as an individual by management, (7) pride in company, (8) satisfaction with salary, (9) attitude toward formal communication system in company, (10) intrinsic job satisfaction, (11) satisfaction with progress and chances for progress, (12) attitude toward co-workers. It is interesting to note that satisfaction is part of morale and contributes to it. Guba (16) has done a study that indicates job satisfaction must be present before morale can be considered as being high. Satisfaction is then a precursor of morale, although it is not possible, as a result of Guba's research, to say it is the most important factor, since other factors were not considered simultaneously. He states that "high morale implies a willingness to engage in activities over and above normal expectations; these obviously require additional energy . . . it follows that states of low satisfaction and high morale are incompatible, for the first saps the energy required by the second" (p. 207). If high morale is to be present, high job satisfaction must also be present because the presence of satisfaction provides additional energy for use in undertaking the pursuit of group goals. An experiment carried out with 168 school teachers substantiated this idea. Learner (26) found the dimensions of morale for 127 naval aviators to be (1) job satisfaction, (2) adjustment to environment, (3) group interactions, (4) professional status values, (5) distribution of work load. The results differ from those of Roach, perhaps because of population differences, but job satisfaction still appears as one of the factors.

An excellent study by Baehr and Renck (1) also revealed job satisfaction as a component of morale. Seventy-six items attempting "to cover all the influences which affect the worker on the job" were put into fourteen categories as follows (p. 161): "(1) job demands, (2) working conditions, (3) pay, (4) employee benefits, (5) friendliness and cooperation of fellow employees, (6) supervisor-employee interpersonal relations, (7) confidence in management, (8) technical competence of supervision, (9) effectiveness of administration, (10) adequacy of communication, (11) security of job and work relations, (12) status and recognition, (13) identification with the company, (14) opportunity for growth and advancement." The items that comprised these categories formed the basis of an employee morale questionnaire. The sample population dealt with involved 400 work groups having a median size of 21.9 and a mean size of 22.5. The composition of the work groups varied from laborers and craftsmen through office workers and professionals to first-line supervision up to top management groups.

A factor analysis of the items produced five factors that accounted for 96.7% of the total variance. The factors (pp. 175–176) are (1) organization and management, "the image of management and the company in the employee's mind," (2) immediate supervision, involving "both the human relations aspect and the purely administrative aspects of the supervisor's job," (3) material rewards, "in terms of pay and in terms of employee benefits," (4) fellow employees, concerning "the friendliness of fellow employees and their ability to work together without friction," (5) job satisfaction, "the intrinsic satisfactions associated with actually doing the job." With the exception of the job satisfaction factor, all these components of morale appear equivalent to the components of job satisfaction as listed in Table 2. The organization and management factor is similar to Kahn's organization-worked-for factor; the immediate supervision factor is similar to the general quality of supervision factor of Stagner, Flebbe, and Wood; material rewards is similar to the financial satisfaction factor of Morse; fellow employees is similar to the co-workers factor of Gadel.

In looking over the other morale studies cited, it is apparent that the correspondence between job satisfaction and morale approaches one-to-one. Two conclusions are readily apparent. First, the naming of the factors is rather subjective and hence while the factors appear semantically the same, they may really differ operationally. The technique of factor analysis, on the other hand, essentially tries to separate out factors, say of morale or satisfaction, and to define them by attaching an appropriate name to each factor. Second, morale and satisfaction are the same because the components of each are the same. Operationally, this must be the case because of equivalent factors. The distinction between the two must be made at the definitional (i.e., semantic) level, reserving the term *satisfaction* for individuals and *morale* for groups. Because the same components apply to both terms, the distinction at present can only be made at this level. Therefore, if an individual displays these factors at a specified level, then he has job satisfaction, and if the group he is in possesses them, the group has morale. Satisfaction and morale are the same in that their components are the same, but they *apply* to different levels within the organization, i.e., individuals and groups.

The Relationship of Morale and Satisfaction to Other Variables

Probably the most discussed aspect of both morale and satisfaction is their relationship to productivity in work. The Katz, Maccoby, and Morse study, mentioned in the section on job satisfaction, found no major relationship between job satisfaction and productivity. Similar results were found by Morse in her *Satisfactions in the White Collar Job* and by

Zalesnik, *et al.* (68). It bears repeating that high productivity will result from high job satisfaction only if the needs a worker has are met by production or if his tensions can be reduced by increased production. A paper by Brayfield and Crockett (7) reviewed the literature on job satisfaction related to productivity up to 1955, and found no significant relationships. A few of their reviews follow. A 1930 study in a Kimberly-Clark mill involving 200-300 girls in routine repetitive jobs showed no relationship between satisfaction on the job and productivity. A 1940 doctoral thesis by Kristy indicated there was no relationship between the two for British post-office clerks. The Life Insurance Agency Management Association in 1947 presented a study showing no relationship for over 6,000 insurance agents. Mossin's 1949 study of 94 teen-age female sales clerks in a department store showed no relationship. An unpublished study by Bellows in 1953 involving 109 male Air Force control tower operators again showed no relationship. In a 1959 symposium of the annual convention of the American Psychological Association, Kahn stated, "I would like to begin by asserting, without qualification, that productivity and job satisfaction do not necessarily go together" (21, p. 275). This summarizes very nicely the research findings relating job satisfaction and productivity.

Concerning morale, Medalia and Miller found for Air Force squadrons of the Air Defense Command that "squadron efficiency is positively associated with squadron morale" (30, p. 351). Such a finding is consistent with the definition of morale, the motivation to work toward a common goal. But this common goal may not always be increased productivity. If high morale is present, the greater the motivation to work for the common goal, and the higher the productivity of the group—if productivity is the group goal. Although this one study does not prove the case, it is expected that morale can be positively related to productivity, by definition. Satisfaction and morale, though measured by the same factors pertain to different levels, with regard to size, in the organization and can, therefore, logically differ in their correlations with the same phenomenon.

Another major relationship is that of satisfaction and morale to absenteeism and job turnover. Morse has said that the "level of general satisfaction may be a predictor of the individual's desire to stay or leave the organization" (33, p. 52); although, she says, this does not mean the individual will definitely leave, for his leaving depends upon the state of the labor market. Similarly, Ross and Zander hypothesize that "workers whose personal needs are satisfied on the job are more likely to remain in the organization" (46, p. 338). They conducted a study involving a number of skilled female workers in a large company and measured their satisfaction on the job. Then, with the passage of time, some of these women left the company. Had their job satisfaction attitudes been measured after they quit, their post-job attitudes would, in all likelihood, affect their recollection of on-job attitudes. The authors also tried "to keep the effects of personal satisfactions on the job independent of the effects of earnings and of the needs which can be met by money" (p. 329) so that the relationships obtained would relate only to personal wants, not to factors excluded from the hypothesis. Their study confirmed this hypothesis and also showed that "on-the-job deprivations and off-the-job interferences are independent social forces upon workers toward resigning" (p. 337). Hence, research in this area should try to hold the off-the-job interferences constant (not at all an easy thing to do) so that turnover is related only to on-the-job satisfactions.

Lindquist studied 284 Swedish factory workers and found "when the worker experiences his work as not being sufficiently independent, as uninteresting or as noisy this tends to induce high absenteeism and turnover" (27, pp. 130-131). The same effect happened when the workers were dissatisfied with their supervision. When the job is not satisfying the wants of the employee, he leaves the job and seeks satisfaction elsewhere. Metzner and Mann found "satisfactions with the work situation were . . . inversely related to absence rates for white collar men working at low skill level jobs and for blue collar men, but not for white collar women or white collar men working at higher level jobs" (32, p. 467). The study involved 163 white collar men and 212 white collar women in the accounting department of a large electric power company and 251 blue collar men, half of them skilled, half unskilled, involved in the maintenance of overhead electric power lines. At the higher skill level jobs, where little correlation exists between satisfaction and absenteeism, the job responsibility is usually higher and preempts any notions of absenteeism. Also, at higher skill levels satisfaction is greater, thus eliminating the possibility of obtaining any kind of a significant relationship through sampling. For the "blue collar men, absences were clearly related to whether the men have a sense of belongingness and group pride" (p. 478); if they did not, they would probably be absent. Generally, at all levels of skill for the white collar workers, significant relationships were found between absences and satisfaction with the supervision and with wages and promotions (p. 478); this latter relationship, though weaker, existed for the blue collar workers also. At the higher skill levels, monetary factors and quality of supervision are more important determinants of satisfaction than, say, work group relations, attitudes toward the company, etc. While these ideas probably hold for women too, the authors suggest that their absences are determined more by off-the-job factors than by on-the-job ones (p. 484). Odiorne (36) found that low satisfaction leads to grievances, turnover, absenteeism and tardiness on the job. In studying 93 industrial organizations, Talacchi (53) found a significant negative relationship between level of satisfaction and absenteeism; this did not apply to turnover rate, since unsatisfied workers apparently do the minimum amount of work to get by with. Mahoney (28) conducted an investigation in a "large military-industrial installation" in Canada and found that low morale was significantly related to absences. In this case, both morale and job satisfaction relate negatively to absences and turnovers, because either group wants or individual wants are not being met; low morale may also cause grievances.

Morale and job satisfaction vary according to age and skill of the worker. In dealing with the age variable, though, the evidence available "suggests that in studying the relationship between age and morale, length of service should be controlled" (4, p. 395). Otherwise, it might be the length of service in the organization that relates to satisfaction, for as the age of the employee increases, so too in all probability does his length of service with the company. Bernberg, in controlling the length of service for 890 aircraft company workers, mostly male, found the older the worker, the higher the morale (4). Gadel, using a sample of 301 women, 60% older than 40, most of them married, doing mostly routine clerical work, found the older women had higher job satisfaction than the younger ones (13, p. 327). Morse also found that older employees are more satisfied with the company (33, p. 78). Those employees with longer service in the company were also more satisfied with the company than were the new employees (33, p. 78). Gadel states "that newly employed older women have much more favorable attitudes toward their jobs than any other group of employees studied" (13, p. 334).

Morse, again, presents an excellent discussion of the age and skill level relationships to morale and satisfaction. "In general, the shorter the time the employee has been with the company the more satisfied he is with his salary and his chances for progress in it" (p. 68). Conversely, the older employees become dissatisfied when their increasing expectations of advancements and salary increases are not met quite so rapidly. "While the average individual who has been in the company a considerable length of time does advance in terms of pay and status, the advancement is not sufficient to be satisfying" (p. 71). All this seems to indicate that there is a positive correlation between job satisfaction and salary level. It has been shown previously, that salary is a component of job satisfaction and morale, but now further analysis is necessary. "The greatest degree of intrinsic job satisfaction occurs among employees performing the most skilled tasks, while the greatest degree of dissatisfaction exists among those doing repetitious clerical work" (p. 56). Hence, skill level is related to job satisfaction. Skill level is also related to salary— the higher the skill level, the higher the salary. Therefore, the apparent relationship of salary to job satisfaction is, in fact, indirect. The higher skill level results in greater job satisfaction at *all* age levels. The older employees are more satisfied with the job content because they have, in most cases, advanced to more skilled jobs. Thus the supervisors are more satisfied than the employees as a whole because the supervisors are generally older and have more highly skilled jobs.

Speroff did a study of 36 men in two small manufacturing plants and "found that no significant relationship exists between worker popularity and job satisfaction" (50, p. 72). As personal popularity has not been shown to be a factor of job satisfaction, such a result is expected. But, another study by Van Zelst, using 66 construction workers who had been working together for at least three months, indicated contrary results. Every worker rated every other worker on a five point scale ranging from (1) "dislike very much" to (5) "like very much." A mean rating given to each worker was computed and correlated with each worker's job satisfaction. The results were, "the popular worker is much more satisfied with his job than the less well-liked employee" (56, p. 410). The author puts the cause and effect relation in doubt, however, by indicating at the time period studied, the workers were in great demand and probably chose their jobs, given equal salaries, on the basis of the pleasantness of working conditions. Therefore, here too, worker popularity is not a component of job satisfaction. Concerning the popularity of a worker's job has in the mind of his family and friends, family disapproval of a job "is more related to satisfaction with the company than with satisfaction with the content of the job itself" (33, p. 51).

Perry and Mahoney used five Minnesota firms (public utility, trucking, wholesale distribution, textile manufacturing, and electrical equipment manufacturing) to study the effects of in-plant communications on job attitudes. The result was that there "is no significant relationship between employees' attitudes toward the company and their knowledge about the company" (37, p. 339). Managerial attempts to increase job satisfaction and morale through the use of in-plant communications about the company appear to be ineffective.) One way of increasing job satisfaction, though, has been shown to be effective by Morse and Reimer: they hypothesized, "an increased role in the decision-making processes for rank-and-file groups increases their satisfaction" (34, p. 120). Using women involved in clerical work in an industrial organization, they proved that decision making satisfied a want, and satisfying this want leads to job satisfaction.

The size of the organization, says Talacchi, "directly affects the individual through changing both the nature of the job and the nature of interpersonal relations on the job" (53, p. 401). In studying 93 industrial companies, his results "indicated that a significant negative relationship existed between size of organization and the . . . general level of employee satisfaction" (p. 409). Similar findings were reported by Meltzer and Salter (31, p. 355) who found the number of levels of management and control in an organization is negatively related to job satisfaction for physiologists throughout the country. Porter (42), using security, social, esteem, autonomy and self-actualization needs, studied 1,916 managers across the country and found "at the Upper-Middle and Vice-President levels, executives in larger companies were clearly more satisfied than their counterparts in smaller companies" (p. 391). However, "managers in bottom levels of smaller companies were more satisfied than managers at the same levels of larger companies" (p. 391). The explanation the author suggests is that the "top manager in a large company controls . . . more people than a top manager in a smaller organization, and hence has . . . more absolute influence in the work situation . . . the worker in the large company has more bosses above him and has less absolute influence on his work environment than does the worker in the small company" (p. 387). Vibert (57) reports when industrial accidents occur, high morale workers attribute the cause of accidents to themselves, while low morale workers attribute the accidents to management's negligence. This seems to be a general halo effect; that is, favorable attitudes toward the group (high morale) lead to favorable attitudes toward things that affect the group, i.e. accidents. Odiorne (36) found that poor equipment maintenance in a company lowered worker job satisfaction because it contributed to poor working conditions, one of the components of job satisfaction.

Supervision, the amount present and its quality, has been shown to be relevant to the attitudes present in job satisfaction and morale. Morse says that the "behavior and attitudes of the immediate supervisors may influence the satisfaction the employee has with his job" (33, p. 46), or alternatively since the cause-effect relations are not clear, satisfaction with the job may produce favorable attitudes toward the supervision. Foa carried out a study in Israel with the officers and crews of 18 ships and found "a stern attitude on the part of the supervisor goes together with lower satisfaction of the worker" (11, p. 161). He administered questionnaires to the crews of the ships in an attempt to measure their expectations of discipline and of satisfaction with the ships' officers and showed that "a certain supervisory attitude might lead to different levels of worker's satisfactions, according to whether such an attitude conforms or not with the expectation of the worker" (p. 161). His findings are consistent with the definition of job satisfaction and since supervision can be considered as a factor of job satisfaction, his results and those of Morse's are also consistent. Porter (41) found that with regard to five needs in Maslow's hierarchy "line managers feel they are more satisfied on their jobs than are staff managers" (p. 274).

In studying the office worker employees of a company that had gone into receivership, Grove found the workers had low job satisfaction even though they had "better pay, superior working conditions, and at least average supervision" as compared with similar employees in other equivalent companies (15). He calls this the result of a halo effect surrounding the bad attitude toward job security. However, this need not be the case because this attitude may simply be stronger than the ones toward pay, working conditions, and the like. This raises an important point: what are the relative weights of each of the components of job satisfaction and morale? If they were known (which they really are not at present), then a multiple regression equation could be written. This would be an equation predicting job satisfaction as a function of its four or five components. It would then be possible to say, for example, that increasing the attitude toward monetary rewards by X amount would have the same effect upon satisfaction as increasing the attitude toward supervision by Y amount. With this equation at hand, different combinations of the components could be used to obtain different levels of satisfaction or morale. Then, if a regression equation could be written to predict labor absences, turnover, and grievances as a function of satisfaction or morale, it could be seen what combination of satisfaction factors would be the most effective in reducing absences, etc. For instance, A amount of the attitude toward the work group, B amount of the attitude toward general working conditions, C amount of the attitude toward the company, etc. would fit in a multiple prediction equation that would define the amount of satisfaction present. Changing these amounts according to the equation could either increase or decrease the satisfaction or keep it the same but with different proportions of the attitudes entering in. In any case, the satisfaction would be brought up to a desired level, using a proper "mix" of the attitudes, to reduce absences according to the relationship established between satisfaction and absences. Such a procedure establishing these relationships would be an important next step in this area.

Job Satisfaction and Morale References

1. Baehr, Melany and Renck, Richard. The definition and measurement of employee morale. *Administrative Science Quarterly* 1958, 3, 157–184.

2. Bernberg, Raymond E. Socio-psychological factors in industrial morale I. *Journal of Social Psychology* 1952, 36, 73–82.

3. ——. Socio-psychological factors in industrial morale II. *Journal of Applied Psychology* 1953, 37, 249–250.

4. ——. Socio-psychological factors in industrial morale III. *Personnel Psychology* 1954, 7, 395–399.

5. Blum, Milton L. *Industrial Psychology and Its Social Foundations*. New York: Harper & Row Publishers, 1956.

6. Brayfield, Arthur H. and Rothe, Harold F. An index of job satisfaction. *Journal of Applied Psychology* 1951, 35, 307–311.

7. —— and Crockett, W. H. Employee attitudes and employee performance. *Psychological Bulletin* 1955, 52, 396–424.

8. ——; Wells, Richard V. and Strate, Marvin W. Inter-relationships among measures of job satisfaction and general satisfaction. *Journal of Applied Psychology* 1957, 41, 201–205.

9. Cureton, Edward E. and Sargent, Byran B. Factor-analytic reanalysis of studies of job satisfaction and morale. *USAF WADD Technical Note* 1960, No. 60–138.

10. Dabas, Zile S. The dimensions of morale: an item factorization of the SRA employee inventory. *Personnel Psychology* 1958, 11, 217–234.

11. Foa, Uriel G. Relation of worker's expectations to satisfaction with the supervisor. *Personnel Psychology* 1957, 10, 161–168.

12. Frisch-Gauthier, Jacqueline. Moral et satisfaction au travail. In *Traite de Sociologie du Travail* by Georges Friedmann and Pierre Naville. Paris: Librairie Armand Colin, 1962.

13. Gadel, Marguerite S. Productivity and satisfaction of full- and part-time female employees. *Personnel Psychology* 1953, 6, 327–342.

14. Gordon, Oakley J. A factor analysis of human needs and industrial morale. *Personnel Psychology* 1955, 8, 1–18.

15. Grove, B. A. and Kerr, W. A. Specific evidence on origin of halo effect in the measurement of employee morale. *Journal of Social Psychology* 1951, 34, 165–170.

16. Guba, Egon G. Morale and satisfaction: a study in past-future time perspective. *Administrative Science Quarterly* 1958, 3, 195–209.

17. Guion, Robert M. Industrial morale I: the problem of terminology. *Personnel Psychology* 1958, 11, 59–64.

18. Herzberg, Fredrick; Mausner, Bernard and Snyderman, Barbara B. *The Motivation to Work*. New York: John Wiley & Sons, Inc., 1959.

19. Hoppock, Robert and Robinson, H. Alan. Job satisfaction researches of 1950. *Occupations* 1951, 29, 572–578.

20. Kahn, Robert L. An analysis of supervisory practices and components of morale. In *Groups, Leadership and Men: Research in Human Relations* by Harold Guetzkow. Pittsburgh: Carnegie Press, 1951.

21. ——. Productivity and job satisfaction. *Personnel Psychology* 1960, 13, 275–287.

22. —— and Katz, Daniel. Leadership practices in relation to productivity and morale. In *Group Dynamics* by Dorwin Cartwright and Alvin Zander. Evanston, Ill.; Row, Peterson & Company, 1960.

23. Katz, Daniel; Maccoby, Nathan and Morse, Nancy C. *Productivity, Supervision, and Morale in An Office Situation.* Ann Arbor: University of Michigan Press, 1950.

24. ——; Maccoby, Nathan; Gurin, Gerald and Floor, Lucretia G. *Productivity, Supervision, and Morale Among Railroad Workers.* Ann Arbor: University of Michigan Press, 1951.

25. Katzell, Raymond A. Measurement of morale. *Personnel Psychology* 1958, 11, 71–78.

26. Learner, David B. Psychological factors of morale. *U.S. Naval School of Aviation Medicine Research Report* 1954, Project No. NM 001058, 21.02, 9.

27. Lindquist, Agne. Absenteeism and job turnover as consequence of unfavorable job adjustment. *Acta Sociologica* 1958, 3, 2–3.

28. Mahoney, Gerald M. Unidimensional scales for the measurement of morale in an industrial situation. *Human Relations* 1956, 9, 3–26.

29. Maslow, A. H. *Motivation and Personality.* New York: Harper & Row Publishers, 1954.

30. Medalia, Nahum Z. and Miller, Delbert C. Human relations leadership and the association of morale and efficiency in work groups. *Social Forces* 1955, 33, 348–352.

31. Meltzer, Leo and Salter, James. Organizational structure and performance and job satisfaction. *American Sociological Review* 1962, 27, 351–362.

32. Metzner, Helen and Mann, Floyd. Employee attitudes and absences. *Personnel Psychology* 1953, 6, 467–485.

33. Morse, Nancy C. *Satisfactions in the White Collar Job.* Ann Arbor: University of Michigan Press, 1953.

34. —— and Reimer, Everett. The experimental change of a major organizational variable. *Journal of Abnormal and Social Psychology* 1956, 52, 120–129.

35. Myers, M. Scott. Who are your motivated workers? *Harvard Business Review* 1964, January-February, 73–88.

36. Odiorne, George S. Some effects of poor equipment maintenance on morale. *Personnel Psychology* 1955, 8, 195–200.

37. Perry, Dallis and Mahoney, Thomas A. In-plant communications and employee morale. *Personnel Psychology* 1955, 8, 339–353.

38. Porter, Lyman W. A study of perceived need satisfactions in bottom and middle management jobs. *Journal of Applied Psychology* 1961, 45, 1–10.

39. ——. Job attitudes in management: I. perceived deficiencies in need fulfillment as a function of job level. *Journal of Applied Psychology* 1962, 46, 375–384.

40. ——. Job attitudes in management: II. perceived importance of needs as a function of job level. *Journal of Applied Psychology* 1963, 47, 141–148.

41. ——. Job attitudes in management: III. perceived deficiencies in need fulfillment as a function of line versus staff type of job. *Journal of Applied Psychology* 1963, 47, 267–275.

42. ——. Job attitudes in management: IV. perceived deficiencies in need fulfillment as a function of size of company. *Journal of Applied Psychology* 1963, 47, 386–397.

43. Roach, Darrell E. Dimensions of employee morale. *Personnel Psychology* 1958 11, 419–431.

44. Robinson, H. Alan and Hoppock, R. A. Job satisfaction researches of 1951. *Occupations* 1952, 30, 594–598.

45. Robinson, H. Alan, *et al.* Job satisfaction researches of 1952 (1953, 1954, 1955, 1956, 1957, 1958, 1959, 1960, 1961). *Personnel and Guidance Journal* 1953 (1954, 1955, 1956, 1957, 1958, 1959, 1960, 1961, 1962), 32 (33, 33, 34, 36, 37, 37, 39, 40, 41), 22–25.

46. Ross, Ian C. and Zander, Alvin. Need satisfactions and employee turnover. *Personnel Psychology* 1957, 10, 327–338.

47. Schaffer, R. H. Job satisfaction as related to need satisfaction in work. *Psychological Monographs* 1953, 67, No. 14.

48. Sinha, Durganand. Job satisfaction in office and manual workers. *Indian Journal of Social Work* 1958, 19, 39–46.

49. Spector, Aaron J. Expectations, fulfillment, and morale. *Journal of Abnormal and Social Psychology* 1956, 52, 51–56.

50. Speroff, B. J. Job satisfaction and interpersonal desirability values. *Sociometry* 1955, 18, 69–72.

51. Stagner, Ross; Flebbe, D. R. and Wood, E. V. Working on the railroad: a study of job satisfaction. *Personnel Psychology* 1952, 5, 293–306.

52. Stagner, Ross. Motivational aspects of industrial morale. *Personnel Psychology* 1958, 11, 64–70.

53. Talacchi, Sergio. Organization size, individual attitudes and behavior. *Administrative Science Quarterly* 1960, 5, 398–420.

54. Triandis, Harry C. A critique and experimental design for the study of the relationship between productivity and job satisfaction. *Psychological Bulletin* 1959, 56, 309–312.

55. Trow, Donald B. Autonomy and job satisfaction in task oriented groups. *Journal of Abnormal and Social Psychology* 1957, 54, 204–209.

56. Van Zelst, R. H. Worker popularity and job satisfaction. *Personnel Psychology* 1951, 4, 405–412.

57. Vibert, P. The presentation of causes of work accidents (in French). *Bulletin du Centre d'Etudes et Recherches Psychotechniques* 1957, 6, 423–428.

58. Viteles, Morris, S. *Motivation and Morale in Industry.* New York: W. W. Norton & Company, Inc., 1953.

59. Vroom, Victor H. Ego-involvement, job satisfaction and job performance. *Personnel Psychology* 1962, 15, 159–178.

60. Walker, Charles R. *Toward the Automatic Factory.* New Haven: Yale University Press, 1957.

61. —— and Guest, Robert H. *The Man on the Assembly Line.* Cambridge: Harvard University Press, 1952.

62. —— and Turner, Arthur N. *The Foreman on the Assembly Line.* Cambridge: Harvard University Press, 1956.

63. Weitz, Joseph and Nuckols, Robert C. Job satisfaction and job survival. *Journal of Applied Psychology* 1955, 39, 294–300.

64. Wherry, Robert J. Factor analysis of morale data: reliability and validity. *Personnel Psychology* 1958, 11, 78–89.

65. Whitlock, Gerald H. The status of morale measurement: 1959. *USAF WADD Technical Note* 1960, No. 60–136.

66. —— and Cureton, Edward E. Validation of morale and attitude scales. *USAF WADD Technical Report* 1960, No. 60–76.

67. Worbis, G. M. Following through on morale studies. *Personnel Psychology* 1958, 11, 89–94.

68. Zalesnik, A.; Christensen, C. R. and Roethlisberger, F. J. *The Motivation, Productivity, and Satisfaction of Workers: A Prediction Study.* Boston: Harvard Business School, 1958.

3 Group Standards

Introduction

Group standards refer to the norms a group sets up, the pressures it uses to enforce these norms, and the concomitant problems of cohesiveness and resistance to change. Academically speaking, psychology has as its unit of analysis the individual, while sociology has as its unit the group, whether it be composed of two people or of a whole society. Strictly speaking, then, this chapter is sociological. Without denying the importance of the individual, it can still be said, from the organizational point of view, that a group is often more important, since a great deal of organizational work is carried out either in formal groups or in larger informal groups.

It has often been stated that a group is more than the sum of its parts, implying it is something more than the individuals in it. Indeed, mass hysteria and mob rule seem to substantiate this conclusion. A group of three people, for example, can wield more power when acting collectively than when acting singly. On the other hand, there are, of course, groups where this does not apply. However, where the group appears to have qualities beyond those of its individual members, norms and cohesiveness are operating to their fullest extent. Norms, says Homans, are "an idea in the minds of the members of a group, an idea that can be put in the form of a statement specifying what the members . . . should do" (33, p. 123). Hare calls them "rules of behavior . . . which have been accepted as legitimate by members of a group" (31, p. 24). Cohesiveness refers to the attractiveness a group has for its members. Therefore, if there is high cohesiveness and the norms are strong for pursuing a particular goal, it would be expected that these two conditions would motivate the members to pursue the goals more fervently than they would if acting alone.

Hare has said the "concern over *norms* and *goals* is the old problem of the *means* and the *ends*, and there is no basis for *organized* interaction in a group until some agreement is reached about each of these kinds of expectations" (31, p. 24). This could be a definition of a group: more than one person united by certain norms and working toward some agreed upon goal. As a group becomes larger, norms become more essential, since greater control is needed with larger numbers of people. Too many norms can prove a detriment, though, and can become so complex that no one can master them. "The result is an unwillingness to act . . . the individual may also become so engrossed with the internal structure and interpretations of the norms that he loses touch with the outside world" (60, p. 140).

Norms can be described in terms of "mechanisms they involve (pressures, sanctions, felt obligations) . . . immediate effects (behavioral uniformity, shared frames of reference) . . . consequences or functions (provision of support for opinions, facilitation of group achievement)" say Thibaut and Kelley (60, p. 126). Therefore, norms create pressures and felt obligations for members of a group—all of which give rise to uniformity of behavior and facilitation of group goals. If, however, a person finds his behavior is deviating from the norms of a group, he can decide either "to conform, to change the norms, to remain a deviant, or to leave the group" (31, p. 24). The person who wishes to change the norms might become the group's new leader; those who leave might form competing groups; and deviants could form competing subgroups working to destroy the group from within.

Group Pressures to Conform

A group often exerts pressures on its members to conform to its norms. Conformity pressures can serve "(a) to help the group accomplish its goals, (b) to help the group maintain itself as a group, and (c) to help the members develop validity or 'reality' for their opinions" (10, p. 169). Exerting social pressure upon individuals keeps the norms constant and preserves the status quo. Compelling them to pursue group goals, facilitated through group norms, ideally makes the path to the goals clearer, and easier. A function a group often serves is the providing of an "audience" with whom a member can exchange opinions. This audience serves as a reality-test for each member's ideas and, in effect, determines whether or not these ideas (or behavior) are realistic for the group. Norms serve to develop similar opinions and behaviors, a universe of discourse in which the opinions expressed are considered realistic and satisfy the members' needs. The attractiveness or cohesiveness the group has for any given individual "depends upon the nature and strength of his needs and upon the perceived suitability of the group for satisfying these needs" (10, p. 72). The more attractive the group is for a person, the greater the power of the group over him and, generally, the more it can force him to conform to its standards. Once a person feels totally accepted by the group, though, he can feel freer "to deviate from the group's standards than do persons who are not certain they are wanted" (10, p. 175). One explanation for this might be that the accepted member is valued for a particular skill which the group would not want to lose. "Members whose deviance in one area is counterbalanced by skills in another area which the group needs may be retained by the group" (31, p. 45).

Asch (3) was one of the first to study the effects of group pressure on individual judgments. The task was to match the length of a line (presented at a distance from the group) with one of three unequal lines presented next to it. In one of his experiments with a group, one of the members was the "subject" and the seven other members were accomplices who were instructed by the experimenter to vote unanimously on an incorrect matching. The subject was made to perceive that by random choice he was to express his judgment last. When the seven accomplices before the subject chose an incorrect matching, Asch found that in many instances the subject agreed with the majority opinion even though it was obviously incorrect. Not everyone was influenced in this matter and there were individual differences. In other experiments, Asch varied the size of the opposing majority. He found "the presence in the field of one other individual who responded correctly was sufficient to deplete the power of the majority, and in some cases to destroy it" (3, p. 195). If the opposition to the subject were only one person, then the subject would not necessarily go against apparent reality. The subject would go along with the majority judgment if the majority consisted of three people; in fact, this majority produced the maximum effect and "majorities of 4, 8, and 16 did not produce effects greater than a majority of 3" (p. 197). Rosenberg (52) used the same experiment and confirmed Asch's result that in a group of two, the subject is not apt to conform. He also found the highest conformity when the majority consisted of 3 people (a four person group). Goldberg (27) performed a similar experiment by having groups attempt to judge the intelligence of persons by their photographs. Before the subject voted on his choice, he was informed of how the others (the accomplices) voted. As with Asch, he found the "knowledge of a group norm by a subject results in the subject's conforming to (reducing his disagreement with) the group norm" (p. 329). He did not find conformity to groups of four to be different from the conformity to groups of two. This does not agree with the previously mentioned studies of Asch and Rosenberg. But in Goldberg's setup, the judgments were made not about an unambiguous thing like length of lines but rather about a very ambiguous thing, intelligence gleaned from photographs. The situations are different, thus it is not surprising there is no absolute agreement on the "optional" size of a majority group to produce conformity.

Milgram (44) used four-man groups, composed of accomplices and two naïve subjects. One of the naïve subjects was to learn a task and the other naïve subject was to administer a shock to him whenever he made a mistake. The two accomplices and this naïve subject were to choose a shock intensity to administer. His results indicate "subjects are induced by the group to inflict pain on another person at a level that goes well beyond levels chosen in the absence of social pressure" (p. 141). Clearly, group pressure can be quite strong.

There is evidence (26, 27) that if conformity is to occur it will occur during the first part of the group life. Goldberg (27) found conformity, if it were to occur at all, developed "within the first few exposures to the group norm" (p. 329). Gerard and Rotter's (26) experiment lasted over a period of four days. Only for the first two days did subjects yield to the majority opinion. In both experiments the conformity was greatest during the first half of the group life. When the time to resolve a conflict in opinion is relatively limited, "the subject displays an all out initial effort to compromise. When this fails after repeated tries, he comes to realize that the others will continue to disagree. The subject therefore begins to revert to his initial private judgments" (26, p. 567).

When a person has to express his opinion publicly rather than privately, as in an Asch-type experiment, he is more likely to conform. Kelley and Volkhart (38) presented a speech to a group of Boy Scouts criticizing their camping activities. Half of them were given a questionnaire to answer concerning their attitudes toward the speech and were told the questionnaire would be made public; the other half were told their responses would be kept secret. The results showed there was a greater agreement with the speaker's opinion for the group told their responses would be made public. Subjects were requested by Argyle (1) to discuss a painting in a two person group. When subjects had to express their opinion directly to the other person, they conformed more with his opinion than when they wrote their opinion down secretly. Raven (50) had stu-

① People tend to adhere closely to group norms a judgments despite
evidence that on a particular issue the group is clearly wrong

40   GROUP STANDARDS

dents discuss possible solutions to a human relations problem and found "the more the individual must communicate regarding the object of opinion, the greater will be the pressure to change his opinion toward the group norm" (p. 123). Furthermore, "the greater the possibility of rejection for nonconformity, the greater the pressure to change toward the group norm" (p. 123). In these face-to-face experiments there is a tendency for a person to deny that he conformed to the group's opinion suggesting "either a greater tendency to maintain 'face' or an actual change in his perceptions due to public pressure" (25, p. 210). In those relatively few cases where an individual publicly expresses an opinion counter to the group's, he becomes quite committed to his opinion and "any change in this behavior in the direction of yielding would violate this [stalwartness] image not only to oneself but to the group" (25, p. 209).

Sherif, White, and Harvey (56) used boys at a summer camp as subjects in an experiment and noted "the higher the status of the member whose performance is judged, the greater the tendency of the others to overestimate his performance" (p. 373); for low status persons there may even be underestimation. Moeller and Applezweig's (45) report on an unpublished study done with college and high school students confirms Sherif's, et al. findings. When the group consisted of low status high school students, college student subjects not only did not conform, but made judgments in the opposite direction, that is, they underestimated the performances of the high school group. When a clearcut leader is present in a group and conformity is studied "it is often difficult to tell whether he is the most 'conforming' or the most 'influential' " (31, p. 41) since he represents group opinion and can either influence it or be influenced by it. As will be pointed out in the leadership chapter, what role the leader plays may depend on at what point in the group's activity he is chosen. If a leader in a problem-solving group is the one who has high achievement in problem solving, then from Nakamura's (46) findings it would be expected that he would not conform, but influence, since there was a "negative correlation between tendency to conform and achievement in problem solving" (p. 318).

There is evidence that conformity behavior is related to needs for social approval. "Students with high motivation for social approval would be more likely to agree with the judgments of their peers" (45, p. 114). Using college students in a different type experiment, Strickland and Crowne conclude "individuals with a high need for social approval will yield to group pressure" (59, p. 177). Relating conformity to education and intelligence, Milgram finds "less educated subjects . . . tended to yield more than those who possess a college degree" (44, p. 141) and DiVesta and Cox report on studies showing "negative correlations between conformity and intellectual ability" (14, p. 266). If intelligence and education are directly related, these two findings complement each other. Apparently, too, older subjects conform less, and female subjects, more often (14 p. 264). Contrasting homogeneous groups (who were told they all had the same skills and knowledge) with heterogeneous groups (who were told they were basically different), Gerard found "greater pressures toward uniformity arose in the homogeneous than in the heterogeneous condition" (24, p. 270), because the homogeneous groups felt that since they were similar in skills, it would be possible to reach an agreement fairly easily. Samelson (53) and Back (4) also found less conformity in heterogeneous groups.

It is clear that more social pressure will eventually produce more conformity (23, 62), but "maximum pressure . . . is required to induce appreciable conformity when material is highly valued" (62, p. 182) or important to an individual. In summary, Gerard states "findings indicate that the magnitude of the pressures toward uniformity is a positive function of: 1. The amount of the discrepancy in opinion that exists. . . . 2. The attractiveness of the group for its members. . . . 3. The importance of the belief or opinion for the functioning of the group" (24, pp. 249–250). There will be great pressure to conform, then, when a highly cohesive group is working toward an important goal or resolving an important issue and faces a large discrepant minority.

In terms of personality, the conforming person "is characterized by restraint, caution, and submissiveness" (14, p. 266). Also, "several investigators have reported that authoritarians are more conforming than are nonauthoritarians" (57, pp. 21–22). Steiner and Johnson's studies were done in such a way that the authoritarian types were confronted by a unanimous group of respected peers. These peers formed an "ingroup" and "to regard the unanimous decision of the ingroup as wrong would be a serious contradiction of the authoritarian's conception of people" (57, p. 22). But in more frequently occurring situations, where there is only a simple majority and not a unanimous opinion to confront the authoritarian, he is probably no more prone to change his views to conform to the group than anyone else. In situational terms, the individual will conform to group opinion "when the object to be judged is ambiguous, if he must make his opinion public, if the majority holding a contrary opinion is large, and if the group is especially friendly or close knit" (31, p. 30). This assumes, of course, that the person is aware his opinions differ from the group's and that the group sets its own standards rather than having them imposed from without.

Cohesiveness

Closely related to the norms of a group is its cohesiveness. It is generally defined as the attraction a group has for its members (4, p. 10). Gross and Martin, however have objected to this definition as it "results in an emphasis on individual perceptions and minimizes the importance of the relational bonds between and among group members" (28, p. 554). The definition presented by Lott (42) satisfies this objection: "cohesiveness is . . . defined as that group property which is inferred from the number and strength of mutual positive attitudes among the members of a group" (p. 279). Only when there is some cohesiveness do group norms take on any meaning, for if the group holds no attraction for its members then informal rules of behavior will probably not be followed, if they develop at all. Conversely, "the more cohesive the group the greater the probability that members will develop uniform opinions and other behaviors" (41, p. 284). Because of the uniformity present in high cohesive groups, Fiedler and Meuwese (21) argue, "cohesive groups probably do not require as much of the leader's effort to maintain the group" (p. 87); the leader can concentrate on goal attainment rather than group maintenance.

Two early experiments in cohesiveness were done by Festinger, et al. (18, 19). They explain the attractiveness of a group in terms of individuals' desires for membership. "Individuals may want to belong to a group because they like other members, because being a member of a group may be attractive in itself . . . or because the group may mediate goals which are important for the members" (19, p. 22). Or in Cartwright and Zander's terms, attractiveness depends on "(a) such properties of the group as its goals, programs, size, type of organization, and position in the community; and (b) the needs of the person for affiliation, recognition, security, and other things which can be mediated by groups" (10, p. 72). The expected value of the attractiveness of a group is called the valence and is "the attractiveness of the group goal, times the probability that the group will reach this goal" (10, p. 75).

Communications play a large part in the concept of cohesiveness. Homans says "if the frequency of interaction between two or more persons increases, the degree of their liking for one another will increase, and vice versa" (33, p. 112), implying communication frequency relates to cohesiveness. As Lott (42) indicates: "the more cohesive the group, the higher the level of communication among the members" (p. 283). Furthermore, Lott hypothesizes cohesiveness will increase "if group members are frequently rewarded in the presence . . . of one another" (p. 282). Since the group as an entity is seen as a distributor of rewards, the attractions of the members to it are natural; these distributions make the members feel accepted. Dittes (13) performed an experiment with college students to establish this hypothesis. One group of subjects was made to feel wanted by being offered monetary rewards for participation and by telling them, to bolster their egos, that a tape of their discussions would be made for further study by social scientists. The remaining groups were given no such special treatment. Dittes then measured each subject's self-esteem and attraction to the group. As expected, the more accepted a person felt, the more he was attracted to the group; this was particularly true for those with low self-esteem, those who had a need for acceptance that the group met. Jackson (35) found for 46 professional people working for a welfare agency in the Midwest, "a person's attraction to membership is directly related to the magnitude of his [perceived] social worth" (p. 324), and this attraction will increase as his social interactions increase.

Lott and Lott studied 15 college student organizations and reported "a group's level of communication [frequency of interaction], and the tendency to conform to the dominant group opinion . . . will be positively related to the degree of cohesiveness present" (41, p. 408). For this reason, conformity is usually expected in high-cohesive groups. As Festinger, et al. have stated, the "greater the cohesiveness of a group . . . the greater will be the amount of influence that can and will be exerted on the members" (19, p. 30). Back (4) obtained similar findings with undergraduates grouped in twos who were asked to write short stories about a group of pictures shown them under conditions of either high or low cohesiveness. "In the highly cohesive groups the discussion was more effective in that it produced influence" (p. 22). That such findings are not the rule Downing (15) showed in an Asch-type experiment using students under high and low cohesiveness conditions. He reports "high-cohesive groups were not more effective than low-cohesive groups in influencing the subjects' judgments" (p. 164). His explanation is that high cohesiveness implies high influence "only where the values of a particular culture [group] sanction such influence" (p. 166). Therefore, for the group to mediate influence there must be a norm, and to have a norm there must be high cohesiveness. By this reasoning, high cohesiveness does not necessarily imply high performance *unless* the norms sanction it. Berkowitz (5) substantiates this with a study of Air Force bomber crews in the Korean War. He found that certain bomber crews who conformed to the group norm and had high cohesiveness did not in fact necessarily do the best possible jobs in a flying mission.

Festinger, Schachter, and Back (18) in studying two married student housing projects at M.I.T. found the more cohesive groups had less deviates or nonconformers in them. The next year Festinger and Thibaut (20) had undergraduates take part in decision-making groups and found "when there is a range of opinion in the group, communications tend to be directed towards those members whose opinions are at the extremes of the range" (p. 99). The rate of communications to these "deviates" increases as the pressures of conformity attempt to bring them back into the mainstream of the group's thinking. Furthermore, the "deviate is rejected more strongly in high- than in low-cohesive groups" (55, p. 198), because he represents a potential threat to cohesiveness. The high-cohesive group is homogeneous in certain respects and has a "natural" aversion to the heterogeneous individual, the deviate. (A "deviate," throughout this discussion, is merely one who does not meet the norms of a particular group; whether the norms are good or bad by society's standards is irrelevant.) Rejection for the deviate comes when he is recognized as one of "those individuals who are identified by their peers as strange, different, atypical, or lacking in prestige at the time they become group members . . . with those individuals who, through inability or lack of motivation, fail to comply with the group's expectations of acceptable behavior" (39, pp. 226–227).

But it is not only the deviate who can threaten the group cohesiveness. Using 16 Naval R.O.T.C. students in four groups of four men each on a reasoning, mechanical assembly, and discussion task, Haythorn (32) found individuals "striving for individual prominence" at the expense of the group could reduce the group cohesiveness. Such persons are not officially deviates; yet they remain threats to the group because they interpret the norms differently.

Consistent with the findings that a high-cohesive group will try to influence deviants from within if the norms so dictate, is the fact that high-cohesive groups express hostility against external threats (49). If cohesiveness precedes the threat to the group hostility toward the external force will develop; but if the threat occurs first, will it affect cohesiveness? Weller (63) has answered in the negative. Using female college students in groups of size 5 to 8 he produced low and high anxiety groups. The high anxiety groups were told they would receive periodic, painful but harmless shocks; the low anxiety groups were told the shocks would be very mild. Groups then discussed human relations problems (problems dealing with human, social interactions). The high anxiety groups did not develop greater cohesiveness because "when threat arises outside the group, the members may not perceive the others as being sources of security and consequently may not have any particular reason to be more attracted to it" (63, p. 196). If the group is cohesive before the threat is presented, the actual presentation of the threat would be met by the group with no expected decrease in cohesiveness and probably with increased cohesiveness. In this instance, the group does become a source of security.

Aronson and Mills designed an experiment to test the "frequent observation that persons who go through a great deal of trouble or pain to attain something tend to value it more highly than persons who attain the same thing with a minimum of effort" (2, p. 177). They used college women and put them into three different groups. But, before the subjects could join their designated group, they had to go through an initiation period. One group had a severe initiation period requiring them to read aloud very embarrassing material. The other group had a milder initiation in reading aloud less embarrassing material. The third group was a control and had no initiation task. After the initiations all groups were asked how desirable they now found group membership. "Subjects who underwent a severe initiation perceived the group as being significantly more attractive than those who underwent a mild initiation or no initiation" (p. 181). The implication would be that cohesiveness increases as the group becomes more difficult to join. When the group goal is clear, that is, when the members know exactly what they are working together for, cohesiveness will also be high (51). If the goal is clear, members can leave the group if they do not like it; a decision to stay means that cohesiveness will be increased through a common goal. "A group will tend to become cohesive if it is formally well organized, the members are individually motivated to do the task, and the group is successful" (31, p. 147). High cohesiveness is a precursor to high morale, for the members must be attracted to the group before they will be motivated to pursue a common goal.

Group Competition and Cooperation

Groups can be involved in decision-making and problem-solving tasks in either a cooperative or a competitive way. It is tacitly assumed in some industrial companies that competition among divisions or smaller sub-groups is "good" for the company. By this, of course, is meant moderate competition that motivates individuals to work harder on a task. But when groups are involved, problems of morale, cohesiveness and norms, which are not present when individuals acting alone are concerned, complicate the results. Deutsch (12) did the first experiment contrasting cooperative and competitive groups. He used college students working on puzzles and human relations problems. He found cooperative groups coordinated their efforts more, were more friendly with each other, and had more productivity per unit time than competitive groups. Similar results were later reported by Grossack (29), Hammond and Goldman (30), and Jones and Vroom (37). Grossack used college women discussing human relations problems and found "cooperative Ss [subjects] showed significantly more cohesive behavior, attempts at influence, exertion and acceptance of pressures toward uniformity" (p. 347). Hammond and Goldman state "non-competition is more favorable for the group process than either group or individual competition" (p. 60). Jones and Vroom explain the productivity advantages of cooperation by the fact that "cooperative conditions are likely to result in a greater division of labor and hence more effective performance" (p. 314). They also point out that where both competitive and cooperative groups have members with preferences to do a particular task, the competitive group's productivity will be hurt the most. Although "even competition requires a minimum of cooperation in establishing and maintaining the rules of the contest" (31, p. 21), it is only in the full cooperation groups that cohesiveness and norms that promote more interaction and greater productivity can develop.

Blake and Mouton (6) formed groups of different sizes as part of a human relations training program and put them in competition with each other. At the end of the decision-making sessions, each group's solution was circulated to the other groups for evaluation. "Group members evaluate their own group product above the judgments they accord to the proposal from a comparison group" (p. 238). Ferguson and Kelley (17) repeated the experiment and found the same results: each "member describes his group's product as superior because he believes he must do so to establish or maintain his good standing in the group" (p. 224). The authors maintain "through participation in producing a particular product, a person sees more of its positive features than does a person who comes to it without the same experience" (p. 224). Apparently, group cohesiveness can account for this "clouding" of judgment. In the Blake and Mouton study 92% of the subjects preferred their group's product (5% regarded it as equal), as contrasted with Ferguson and Kelley's finding that 55% preferred their group's product (23% regarded it as equal). There is not complete numerical agreement because the experimental conditions were somewhat different, but the findings are in the right direction.

Resistance to Change

Change is something that goes on in all long-term groups and organizations; it may be a change of goals, means to these goals, personnel, or just a change of interests and opinions of the group members. Major changes may take place in groups that keep the status quo as a goal, but minor changes are inevitable. Not everyone regards change as favorable because it requires some modification of behavior patterns. Factory workers can feel any change in their work will affect their wages or security. Even a change such as an executive promotion can lead to doubts about the new responsibilities and social interactions that will develop. The *net* attitude toward change may, of course, be favorable, but chances are there are some unfavorable components present. In short, change involves something unknown—and is accepted with reservation.

Automation probably accounts for the largest changes in factory and office work. Bright (8) argues that automation lowers skill requirements in industry. His observations are based on 50,000 workers in 13 plants. He points out that both mental effort and physical effort decrease as mechanization increases since the machine does most of the decision making. Physical effort is also taken out of the worker's hands by the machine. In a kind of chain reaction, education and training also fall off. The effects of automation upon the social structure in a plant has been reported by Faunce (16). He interviewed 125 workers in four machine departments in an automated engine plant in Detroit. All of the workers he interviewed were transferred to this new plant from an older one. In the new plant, there was less team work needed and less social interaction among them. Old working groups were effectively broken up; new norms had to be formed, and cohesiveness redeveloped. The effects of change upon white collar workers has also been studied (34, 36, 40, 43). Changes in the organizational structure usually accompany the installation of electronic data processing systems, since computers replace most of the lower-level decision makers. Norms and cohesiveness must change with the introduction of more automation—if for no other reason than that individuals are reorganized into other groups. If when the new norms are developed, they are the result of resentment to the changes, then the organization's goal pursuit can be blocked. That is, new groups with new norms can develop and have as their goal the hindrance of organizational objectives.

Most people gradually become accustomed to change. Unions as a force of change were not widely accepted in the 1920's, but in the 1950's they were, in principle. Negroes who were introduced into white departments in a Chicago meat-packing plant were strongly resented at first, but after a time the initial hostility toward them diminished (47). As Coch and French (11) found out, if the change is introduced "correctly," resistance can be minimized. Their study took place in a pajama factory in the South. The company had had good labor relations and tried to accommodate its workers; but when it attempted to transfer workers from one job to another, it met resistance in the form of lower productivity. Initial low productivity was anticipated, but after the learning period the workers transferred to this task continued to produce less than the original workers. As an experiment Coch and French formed three groups of workers. The control group had their jobs changed as before, with no participation with management in the transfer arrangements. The second group chose representatives to discuss with management any changes they might be involved in. The third group had total participation with management. Then all groups were given their new assignments. The control group showed the same resistance to change as was found before. But the total participation group reached the production standard the quickest, followed by the representation group. Therefore, it was concluded that "participative management," the discussion with management by the employees about proposed changes, was effective in reducing resistance to change. Under the conditions with no participative management, the work groups purposely restricted their production—a group norm in protest to the change. Becoming an integral part of that change was an effective device to lessen their protest and to suggest group norms in compliance with management policy. French, *et al.* (22) introduced further changes ten years later via participative management techniques and found very little resistance to change. "The important element in change is not so much having a chance to discuss the problem as it is providing an effective method for breaking down the old value system before adopting a new one" (31, p. 47).

Persons lowest in the hierarchy are often affected the most by change and are often the most resistant to it. The lower-level personnel are remote "both in position and identification, from the professional goal-setters of the institution. At the same time, a great deal of reliance is placed on them for the achievement of the institution's goals" (48, p. 334). Thus, it is important that resistance be overcome in such a way that both management and employees benefit. If there is resistance, productivity is reduced and management suffers. If too much pressure is applied on the employee to change, he can quit his job, thereby delaying the achievement of the organization's goals. "Change is an integral and essential part of all organization behavior" (54, p. 67), and it is important, therefore, that it be carried on as effectively as possible. As Stewart (58) points out, resistance operates on two levels: resistance to the change itself, which is unavoidable, and resistance to the method of introduction, which may be circumvented.

Trumbo's (61) study of supervisors and their subordinates in an insurance company reveals a positive correlation between the supervisor's attitudes toward change and the subordinate's. He found a negative correlation between group cohesiveness and favorable attitudes toward change because change poses a threat to the group's structure; the more cohesive the group, the more it has to lose vis-á-vis its attractiveness. The leadership and the norms a group has can and do affect attitudes toward change. Some principles of change introduction have been listed by Cartwright (9). "Those people who are to be changed, and those who are to exert influence for change must have a strong sense of belonging to the same group" (p. 388). If both parties perceive they are working for the same end then an element of trust is present that serves to reduce barriers. "Efforts to change . . . which, if successful, would have the result of making them deviate from the norms of the group will encounter strong resistance" (p. 389). Group norms are powerful and resist attempts at change. However, if the group can be made to see the need for a change, the pressure for change will come from within the group (p. 390). If the leader of the group is convinced of the need for change he can exert his influence to help make the change come from within (p. 389). Participative management approaches these principles in order to introduce change effectively. In fact, effective group change can only come from within.

GROUP STANDARDS REFERENCES

1. Argyle, M. Social pressure in public and private situations. *Journal of Abnormal and Social Psychology* 1957, 54, 172–175.

2. Aronson, Elliot and Mills, Judson. The effect of severity of initiation on liking for a group. *Journal of Abnormal and Social Psychology* 1959, 59, 177–181.

3. Asch, S. E. Effects of group pressure upon the modification and distortion of judgments. In *Group Dynamics* edited by Dorwin Cartwright and Alvin Zander. Evanston, Ill.: Row, Peterson & Company, 1960.

4. Back, Kurt W. Influence through social communication. *Journal of Abnormal and Social Psychology* 1951, 46, 9–23.

5. Berkowitz, Leonard. Group norms among bomber crews: Patterns of perceived crew attitudes, "actual" crew attitudes, and crew liking related to aircrew effectiveness in Far Eastern combat. *Sociometry* 1956, 19, 141–153.

6. Blake, Robert R. and Mouton, Jane S. Overevaluation of own group's product in intergroup competition. *Journal of Abnormal and Social Psychology* 1962, 64, 237–238.

7. Boomer, Donald S. Subjective certainty and resistance to change. *Journal of Abnormal and Social Psychology* 1959, 58, 323–328.

8. Bright, James R. Does automation raise skill requirements? *Harvard Business Review* 1958, 36, July-August, 85–98.

9. Cartwright, Dorwin. Achieving change in people: some applications of group dynamics theory. *Human Relations* 1951, 4, 381–392.

10. —— and Zander, Alvin. *Group Dynamics.* Evanston, Ill.: Row, Peterson & Company, 1960.

11. Coch, Lester and French, John R. P., Jr. Overcoming resistance to change. *Human Relations* 1948, 1, 512–532.

12. Deutsch, Morton. An experimental study of the effects of co-operation and competition upon group process. *Human Relations* 1949, 2, 199–231.

13. Dittes, James E. Attractiveness of group as function of self-esteem and acceptance by group. *Journal of Abnormal and Social Psychology* 1959, 59, 77–82.

14. DiVesta, Francis J. and Cox, Landon. Some dispositional correlates of conformity behavior. *The Journal of Social Psychology* 1960, 52, 259–268.

15. Downing, John. Cohesiveness, perception and values. *Human Relations* 1958, 11, 157–166.

16. Faunce, William A. Automation in the automobile industry: some consequences for in-plant social structure. *American Sociological Review* 1958, 23, 401–407.

17. Ferguson, Charles K. and Kelley, Harold H. Significant factors in overevaluation of own-group's product. *Journal of Abnormal and Social Psychology* 1964, 69, 223–228.

18. Festinger, Leon; Schachter, Stanley and Back, Kurt. *Social Pressures in Informal Groups.* New York: Harper & Row Publishers, 1950.

19. ——; Back, Kurt; Schachter, Stanley; Kelley, Harold H. and Thibaut, John. *Theory and Experiment in Social Communication.* Ann Arbor, Michigan: Research Center for Group Dynamics, University of Michigan, 1950.

20. —— and Thibaut, John. Interpersonal communication in small groups. *Journal of Abnormal and Social Psychology* 1951, 46, 92–99.

21. Fiedler, Fred E. and Meuwese, W. A. T. Leader's contribution to task performance in cohesive and uncohesive groups. *Journal of Abnormal and Social Psychology* 1963, 67, 83–87.

22. French, J. R. P., Jr.; Ross, I. C.; Kirby, S.; Nelson, J. R. and Smyth, P. Employee participation in a program of industrial change. *Personnel* 1958, 35, No. 3, 16–29.

23. ——; Morrison, H. William and Levinger, George. Coercive power and forces affecting conformity. *Journal of Abnormal and Social Psychology* 1960, 61, 93–101.

24. Gerard, Harold B. The effect of different dimensions of disagreement on the communication process in small groups. *Human Relations* 1953, 6, 249–271.

25. ——. Conformity and commitment to the group. *Journal of Abnormal and Social Psychology* 1964, 68, 209–211.

26. —— and Rotter, George S. Time perspective, consistency of attitude, and social influence. *Journal of Abnormal and Social Psychology* 1961, 62, 565–572.

27. Goldberg, Solomon C. Three situational determinants of conformity to social norms. *Journal of Abnormal and Social Psychology* 1954, 49, 325–329.

28. Gross, Neal and Martin, William E. On group cohesiveness. *American Journal of Sociology* 1952, 57, 546–554.

29. Grossack, Martin M. Some effects of cooperation and competition upon small group behavior. *Journal of Abnormal and Social Psychology* 1954, 49, 341–348.

30. Hammond, Leo K. and Goldman, Morton. Competition and non-competition and its relationship to individual and group productivity. *Sociometry* 1961, 24, 46–60.

31. Hare, A. Paul. *Handbook of Small Group Research.* New York: Free Press of Glencoe, Inc., 1962.

32. Haythorn, William. The influence of individual members on the characteristics of small groups. *Journal of Abnormal and Social Psychology* 1953, 48, 276–284.

33. Homans, George C. *The Human Group.* New York: Harcourt, Brace & World, Inc., 1950.

34. Hoos, Ida R. The sociological impact of automation in the office. *Management Technology* 1960, 1, No. 2, 10–19.

35. Jackson, Jay M. Reference group processes in a formal organization. *Sociometry* 1959, 22, 307–327.

36. Jacobson, Eugene; Trumbo, Don; Cheek, Gloria and Nangle, John. Employee attitudes toward technological change in a medium sized insurance company. *Journal of Applied Psychology* 1959, 43, 349–354.

37. Jones, Stephen C. and Vroom, Victor H. Division of labor and performance under cooperative and competitive conditions. *Journal of Abnormal and Social Psychology* 1964, 68, 313–320.

38. Kelley, Harold H. and Volkhart, E. H. The resistance to change of group-anchored attitudes. *American Sociological Review* 1952, 17, 453–465.

39. Kidd, John W. An analysis of social rejection in a college men's residence hall. *Sociometry* 1951, 14, 226–234.

40. Kraut, Allen I. How EDP is affecting workers and organizations. *Personnel* 1962, 39, No. 4, 38–50.

41. Lott, Albert J. and Lott, Bernice E. Group cohesiveness, communication level, and conformity. *Journal of Abnormal and Social Psychology* 1961, 62, 408–412.

42. Lott, Bernice E. Group cohesiveness: a learning phenomenon. *The Journal of Social Psychology* 1961, 55, 275–286.

43. Mann, Floyd C. and Williams, Lawrence K. Observations on the dynamics of a change to electronic data-processing equipment. *Administrative Science Quarterly* 1960, 5, 217–256.

44. Milgram, Stanley. Group pressure and action against a person. *Journal of Abnormal and Social Psychology* 1964, 69, 137–143.

45. Moeller, George and Applezweig, Mortimer H. A motivational factor in conformity. *Journal of Abnormal and Social Psychology* 1957, 55, 114–120.

46. Nakamura, Charles Y. Conformity and problem solving. *Journal of Abnormal and Social Psychology* 1958, 56, 315–320.

47. Palmore, Erdman B. The introduction of negroes into white departments. *Human Organization* 1955, 14, No. 1, 27–28.

48. Pearlin, Leonard I. Sources of resistance to change in a mental hospital. *American Journal of Sociology* 1962, 68, 325–334.

49. Pepitone, Albert and Reichling, George. Group cohesiveness and the expression of hostility. *Human Relations* 1955, 8, 327–337.

50. Raven, Bertram H. Social influence on opinions and the communication of related content. *Journal of Abnormal and Social Psychology* 1959, 58, 119–128.

51. —— and Rietsema, Jan. The effects of varied clarity of group goal and group path upon the individual and his relation to his group. *Human Relations* 1957, 10, 29–45.

52. Rosenberg, Leon A. Group size, prior experience, and conformity. *Journal of Abnormal and Social Psychology* 1961, 63, 436–437.

53. Samelson, Franz. Conforming behavior under two conditions of conflict in the cognitive field. *Journal of Abnormal and Social Psychology* 1957, 55, 181–187.

54. Sayles, Leonard R. The change process in organizations: an applied anthropology analysis. *Human Organization* 1962, 21, 62–67.

55. Schachter, Stanley. Deviation, rejection, and communication. *Journal of Abnormal and Social Psychology* 1951, 46, 190–207.

56. Sherif, Muzafer; White, B. Jack and Harvey, O. J. Status in experimentally produced groups. *American Journal of Sociology* 1955, 60, 370–379.

57. Steiner, Ivan D. and Johnson, Homer H. Authoritarianism and conformity. *Sociometry* 1963, 26, 21–34.

58. Stewart, Michael. Resistance to technological change in industry. *Human Organization* 1957, 16, No. 3, 36–39.

59. Strickland, Bonnie R. and Crowne, Douglas P. Conformity under conditions of simulated group pressure as a function of the need for social approval. *The Journal of Social Psychology* 1962, 58, 171–181.

60. Thibaut, John W. and Kelley, Harold H. *The Social Psychology of Groups.* New York: John Wiley & Sons, Inc., 1959.

61. Trumbo, Don A. Individual and group correlates of attitudes toward work-related change. *Journal of Applied Psychology* 1961, 45, 338–344.

62. Vaughan, G. M. and Mangan, G. L. Conformity to group pressure in relation to the value of the task material. *Journal of Abnormal and Social Psychology* 1963, 66, 179–183.

63. Weller, Leonard. The effects of anxiety on cohesiveness and rejection. *Human Relations* 1963, 16, 189–197.

64. Wolman, Benjamin B. Impact of failure on group cohesiveness. *The Journal of Social Psychology* 1960, 51, 409–418.

4 Decision Making

Introduction

Decision making merely involves making a choice among alternatives. An individual or a group searches among the alternatives present and decides on a course of action. The simplest situation is a binary one, either take some particular action or take no action. In some cases, the alternatives to choose from may be infinite, in which case certain boundaries on feasibility must be established, i.e., some alternatives must be eliminated, so that a denumerable listing of alternatives is possible. It may be that specific results can be attached to each of the possible alternatives but usually some amount of haziness surrounds the outcome as well as the feasible or possible courses of action. Ideally, the choice of an action would be optimal, the best possible, but most decisions cannot be judged on this optimality basis because there seldom exists an optimality criterion. Such a criterion would enable the decision makers to compare each alternative's result with the optimal result, but the results of most decisions are not known until after the decision is actually made. This is to say, all decisions must be made simultaneously and independent of each other and after observing all the results, a *best* decision is chosen. Obviously, this is impossible.

Statistical decision theory is one approach to decision making that is limited to highly structured situations where the costs and rewards of decision making, choosing a course of action, are quite explicit and can be formulated mathematically. Basically, the concern is with statistical problems of parameter estimation, hypothesis testing, etc. In the mathematical area of decision making there is also operations research, which is, essentially, the application of mathematics to such industrial problems as inventory and production control, resource allocation, etc. The problem here is to choose economic policies that usually either minimize costs or maximize profits. A paper by Dean (15) presents a fine nontechnical exposition of operations research and its relationship to managerial decision making. This kind of mathematical decision making is, with few exceptions to be noted, divorced from the characteristics of human behavior and for this reason will not be discussed further. While game theory does involve human behavior (69a), the decisions can be made *against* an opponent who can also make choices against the other player. Decision making, on the other hand, does not have immediate potentially negative consequences to another. The role of decision-making in behavioral science is to describe how people make decisions under conditions of imperfect information—that is, where complete information as to the present state of affairs, possible courses of action, and consequences is not available. Decisions are influenced by individual differences, social pressures, leadership differences, communication structures, etc. Social scientists are interested in how individuals and groups reach a decision; how much information is necessary, who influences the outcome the most, how disagreements are resolved, what procedures are used, and how choices are made. Since the kind of decision making relevant to behavioral science covers such a broad area, many different categories of decision making are possible: quantitative, qualitative; normative, substantive; those based upon the functions of decision making, and those based upon its determinants.

However, this chapter will present decision making in three categories: *intra-organizational decision making, problem solving,* and *individual choice behavior.* Intra-organizational decision making involves the general aspects of decision making within an organization and the choosing of courses of action as influenced by certain variables. Problem solving refers, not to general decision making, but to attempts on the part of individuals and groups to solve specific problems. The choice of alternatives is among solutions rather than among possible courses of action. Individual choice behavior, while consisting of choosing courses of action, has a different focus from intra-organizational decision making because of its unique development—mathematical or metric and economic, dealing with utility and probability preferences. Unfortunately, the correspondence between the research on individual choice behavior and its applicability to organizational decision-making has not been close. However, the research does deal with the variability of human behavior; inferences from it to possible behavioral patterns in organizational decision making can be made with caution. This same difficulty arises in the problem-solving section, for here, too, the studies are conducted outside an economic, military, or governmental organization. Groups in a social science laboratory could be termed organizations and their behavior analyzed on this basis. But a more reasonable attitude is to acknowledge that the problems these people are trying to solve are not the same as those existing organizations deal with; then results can be transferred to real-life situations with caution.

Organizations and the people within them solve different problems and make different choices than laboratory groups usually do, but it is expected that the ways of making decisions in all contexts have some fundamental principles in common. Statistically speaking, the most difficult problem here is inferring from a laboratory group of college students solving mathematical puzzles to a real organization solving economic problems. Not only is the population different, but so also is the task. However, if there are "universal" principles of decision making, the inference errors will be much less serious. Whether or not universals exist appears to be largely a philosophical question; but if human behavior can be likened to natural and physical phenomena, it is reasonable to assume such principles do exist. Therefore, aspects of human decision making (problem solving, choice behavior, etc.) having behavioral components or variables will be discussed without restricting discussion to real-life situations—although the emphasis will be on the relevance to organizations existing as part of our society.

Decision making in its total meaning not only includes many different components but also relates to several other areas of organizational behavior. As an example of these interrelations, Wasserman and Silander's (85) annotated bibliography is divided into the following categories: decision-making process, values and ethical considerations, leadership as a factor in decision making, psychological factors, decision making in small groups, community decision making, communications and information handling, and mathematics and statistics in decision making. This complexity can be summed up in a behavioral sense by stating, as Gore and Silander have, that there is "no question but that the configuration of shared values, the structure of roles that set the relationships between individuals in the group, the reward and penalty systems, the mechanisms of social control, the division of labor, and the technology of a group all have considerable impact upon its decision-making processes" (32, p. 107). The concern will be with how all this relates to the decision-making process.

Intra-organizational Decision Making

In a situation where there are several problem solutions rather than just one, the choice of a solution is the important thing to consider. The choices involve the decision making. Specifically with regard to an administrative process, Litchfield lists five subactivities of decision making. When administrative decision making is rational and purposive it involves: "definition of the issue . . . analysis of the existing situation . . . calculation and delineation of alternatives . . . deliberation . . . choice" (43, pp. 13–14). This is a straightforward but by no means definitive statement on the process. Brim, Glass, Lavin and Goodman list six phases of the decision process for parents deciding how to raise their children: "identification of the problem . . . obtaining the necessary information . . . production of possible solutions . . . evaluation of such solutions . . . selection of a strategy for performance . . . actual performance" (8, p. 9). Actually, Litchfield and Brim, et al., are saying the same thing, only in different words. Again, Tannenbaum breaks the managerial decision-making process into recognition of behavior alternatives, formulation of the consequences of each alternative, and evaluation of the alternatives (72, p. 24). This is a simplified version of what the others have said; the general idea of the process is agreed upon but the details vary somewhat. Obviously, one must first have a decision to make; then listing alternative actions and their possible consequences leads to a selection of an alternative. What specific steps to follow depend on the situation, as Brim et al. (8, p. 10) point out; if an action is desired, the decision must be effectively communicated and, if necessary, kept up to date. "Decisions are based on facts, assumptions, and values which are subject to change . . . decisions must therefore be reviewed and revised as rapidly as change occurs" (43, p. 19).

From observations of decision making and problem solving in ten organizations, Bakke (4, pp. 62–66) lists 11 steps involved in selecting an acceptable course of action: (1) "Awareness" of the problem or situation, (2) "Exploration" of the problem to gather relevant information as to the cause and impact and involvement of the problem, (3) "Structuring"—making accurate judgments about the exploration phase, (4) "Simplification" of the problem so it can easily be dealt with, (5) "Search and Cue" for alternatives, (6) "Appraisal of Alternatives," (7) "Choice and Decision," (8) "Mobilization" of necessary resources for solution of the problem, (9) "Response and Action" to carry out the objectives of the decision making, (10) "Experience and judgment" of the solution, and (11) "Closure"—a check to see if the problem is actually solved. These steps differ, again, only slightly from the ones others have listed.

Rather general behavior has been described that appears to fit most, if not all, decision-making and problem-solving situations. A more specific set of behaviors, for the decision making of government executives, has been determined by Forehand and Guetzkow (30). Their study involved 127 government executives in 27 United States Government agencies. These officials' decision-making behavior was determined by having one peer and one superior rate each of the officials on 39 different behavior description scales. About half of these scales dealt with the "context of the decision-making situation" and the remaining dealt with "characteristics of his decision-making style." The traits or behavior that emerged from the analysis of the completed description scales were (pp. 362–366): (1) *self-confidence* in making decisions, (2) *cautiousness*—attention paid to broad implications of decisions, (3) *discernment*—consideration of subtle aspects of a situation, (4) *prudence,* (5) *analytic decision-making capability*—intellectual and systematic analysis of decisions to be made, (6) *bureaucratic decision-making capability*—following rules and previous policy guides and developing group agreement, (7) *policy making abilities,* including using policy already set up, (8) *policy execution abilities*—ability to carry out policies. Unfortunately, this may not be the true behavior of the officials and may only reflect the perceptions of their behavior by their peers and superiors (p. 369). Furthermore, these traits are a function of the 39 behavior description scales they were derived from. Since the officials knew they were being rated on possible behaviors, the ratings may only measure those decision-making actions made in the presence of peers and subordinates; they may be either distorted or part of a larger set of behaviors. But if this behavior is generally accurate, it would apply to most bureaucratic decision makers who must follow pre-established organizational procedures.

Business executives are always making economic and social decisions that usually "depend on information, estimates, and expectations that ordinarily differ appreciably from reality" (13, p. 83). In attempting to develop a behavioral theory of the firm, Cyert and March (13, p. 126) have developed a scheme they feel represents the organizational decision process. Figure 1, a slight modification of this scheme, indicates a subunit's (department's) decision-making procedure for reaching a particular goal. The decision-making unit observes the environment and notes down information about the desired goal. If this information is too uncertain, more is gathered. If it is seen that the desired goal is not being achieved, a search is made in the local environment to determine the nature of the problem; the search is expanded if necessary. When the problem is found, the ways of finding and solving the problem are evaluated to arrive at a set of decision rules to be used should the same problem arise again. The decision makers are, then, structuring problematical situations in such a way that the organization can handle them in its own way using standardized procedures. The goals are evaluated and the process continues.

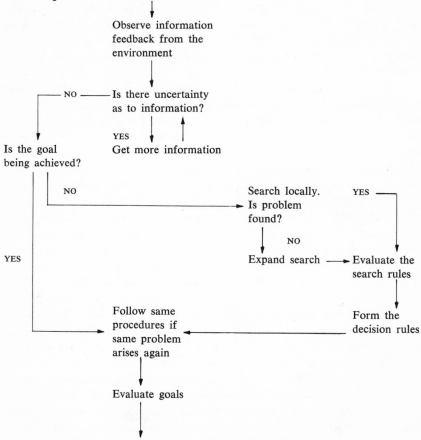

Figure 1. The organizational decision process for reaching a specific goal. (Modified from Richard M. Cyert and James G. March, *A Behavioral Theory of the Firm.* © 1963. Reprinted by permission of Prentice-Hall, Inc.)

Obtaining accurate information for the decision processes is quite important, but, unfortunately, biases are sometimes unavoidable. Cyert and March (13) have conducted an experiment revealing the origin of biases. Different groups of graduate students played the roles of men in companies estimating sales and production costs for a new product. The estimates were made from a single set of numbers shown to both those in the cost estimating role and those in the sales estimating role. It was found that the "sales" people underestimated the numbers and the "cost" people overestimated (p. 70). The explanation is that there was a biased payoff structure operating—that is, the payoff was perceived by either group of estimators to be larger in one direction than in the other. For instance, salesmen will tend to underestimate sales because they feel that when actual sales go above this estimate, their payoff or reward from management will increase. While if they overestimated sales, they would feel management would attribute this "decrease" in sales to them. Production men overestimate costs, then, because they feel their payoff from management will be greater in this direction.

Several experiments have been performed that relate the amount of information a group possesses to the group's decision-making performance. Shaw and Penrod (67) performed three sets of experiments with all male and all female groups discussing case studies of a human relations nature, i.e., personal interactions of some sort. In Experiment I, Condition 1, all three members of the group were given one paragraph as the case study, one question to answer and five possible solutions. This was the control group not only for Experiment I, but also for Condition 1 for Experiments II and III. For Experiment I, Condition 2, one member of the group was given a second paragraph pertaining to the case study, that is, he was given additional task-relevant information but was not to tell anyone he had such extra information. However, he could use the information to help his group solve its problem. For Condition 3, this same person was given still another extra paragraph with the same restrictions on revealing its source. The results for Experiment I suggest "that additional information held by one member of the group does not necessarily improve . . . the quality of group decisions" (67, p. 385). It is possible the special member in the group was not able to get his information communicated effectively to the group; since he could not validate the source of his information, the group rejected it, thinking, perhaps, that he only thought he had some extra information.

In Experiment II, Condition 2 involved giving the first extra paragraph to all members of the group and Condition 3 involved giving the second extra paragraph to all members. It was found that in both conditions the extra information reduced the solution time, but only in Condition 3 was the solution better than those obtained in Experiment I. For the different Conditions of Experiment III, only one person was given the extra information, but this time the group knew someone would have the extra information. The results showed, however, no improvement in the quality of the solution chosen. Obviously, different groups were involved in the three experiments and all additional information should have increased the quality of the solutions, but generally it did not!

A similar experiment was performed by Shaw (6) on seven groups of three undergraduates discussing human relations problems. Depending on the conditions of the experiment, one of the group members was given either 2, 4 or 6 possible solutions to the problem but, as before, could not reveal the source of the extra information. The results showed "no differences in the 'quality' of solution as a function of the amount of information possessed" (66, p. 76) by the group. It appeared that when the informed person had 6 possible solutions at his disposal, he did not emphasize one solution over the others. This switching from one solution to another made the group feel he was uncertain about his information. As Shaw and Penrod have suggested, "with moderate amounts of additional information a group member's influence upon the group is increased and the group's performance is improved . . . with greater amounts . . . the reverse is true" (67, p. 390).

In inferring these experimental results to decision-making groups in general, it can be said that the most knowledgeable member of a group is not necessarily the most influential in the problem-solving process, probably for several reasons: he may not effectively communicate his extra knowledge to the group; his additional information may not have sufficient authority for the group to accept it as legitimate. Torrance (79) in studying three-person groups of pilots, navigators, and gunners found that status differences among these people accounted for acceptance of rather poor decisions. That is, poor suggestions by pilots were accepted more often than good ones by gunners, who were of a lower status. Riecken (62) has demonstrated that the most influential group member is the one who does the most talking. He had 32 groups of 4 undergraduates each discuss two human relations problems and from the discussions, picked out the most talkative (top) and least talkative (bottom) individuals in each group. For a new human relations problem, the most talkative member in some groups was given the solution to the problem, and the least talkative in the remaining groups—unknown, of course, to the other group members. When the top man has the solution information, "the group accepts this solution more than two-thirds of the time; when the bottom man has the same information, the . . . solution is rejected in more than two-thirds of the groups" (62, p. 313). As a word of explanation, Riecken says that "perhaps the participants in a discussion confound quantity with quality in such a way that the greatest talker is also seen as making the best contribution" (p. 316). As the top and bottom men had about the same intelligence, it does appear that the amount of talking is the important variable. In the cases where the high talkers did not have

status is an important asset when trying to get a group to accept your recommendations

their solutions accepted, it was probably because they did not personally support the solution given them.

It has been shown by Ziller and Behringer (89) that the past performance of a group determines just how it will receive a newcomer to the group. They used 120 undergraduates in 40 three-person groups to solve two problems via a note-passing scheme between group members. That is, this was not a face-to-face problem-solving session, but one in which the problem solving was done by passing written messages between the group members. Depending on the experimenters' choice, some groups were told they had succeeded on the two problems and the other groups were told they had failed. One new person was added to each group under the pretext that the experimenters wanted to observe the effect on problem solving of increasing group size—in fact, each newcomer had the solution to the problem the group was to work on next; the new problem was such that it could only be solved with the extra information the newcomer possessed. It was found that those groups who were told they previously "failed" solved the problem more often than those who were told they previously "succeeded." The "failure" groups solved more because they were influenced by the newcomer. "Unsuccessful groups . . . may be expected to perceive the newcomer as a possible resource and as an agent or catalyst of change" (89, p. 288). On the other hand, "to a successful group, the newcomer represents a potentially disruptive force threatening to stimulate changes" (p. 288).

The phenomenon of cognitive dissonance applies to the information accuracy that is needed in decision making. This theory "predicts that, following a decision, a person will attempt to convince himself that the chosen alternative is even more attractive (relative to the unchosen one) than he had previously thought" (29, p. 215). Furthermore, "the greater the number of alternatives among which a person must choose [and] . . . the greater the qualitative dissimilarity between the alternatives . . . the greater would be the post-decision dissonance" (29, p. 216). In support of this, two studies will be cited. Mills, Aronson, and Robinson (57) gave undergraduates a choice of two examinations to take: one an essay exam, the other an objective one. The students were presented with a list of six different articles, three about essay exams and three about objective ones, either supporting or rejecting the particular type of exam. It was found that when an article agreed with the subject's choice of an exam, he would choose that article to read. Ehrlich, Guttman, Schonback, and Mills (26) studied 60 new car owners and found "that new car owners read advertisements of their own car more often than of cars they considered but they did not buy" (p. 101).

The relationship of information to decision making has been dealt with in quite another way by an approach called the "economic theory of

A person making a decision will afterwards become a fierce advocate of that decision, even if he was originally hesitant about it.

62 DECISION MAKING

teams" or "team decision theory." Marschak has defined a team as "a group of people each of whom makes decisions about something different but who receive a common reward as the joint result of all those decisions" (55, p. 128). That is, a team is a group of people working together for a common reward of some sort. The team decision problem is how to choose the best decision rules for alternate courses of action given certain communication structures and costs of communication. Marschak (55, p. 133) presents six simple communication networks involving two separate decision makers and their information on two particular events that they should act together on. If decision maker I observes no event and decision maker II observes no event, and if there is no communication between them, then obviously neither of them will act and the relative success of their decision is zero. If I observes the event he is closest to and communicates it to II who does not observe the event he is closest to, then both I and II have information on the same event and the relative success of their decision to act is higher than before—they are acting on partial information. Their joint decision to act would be optimal if both I and II observed the event closest to him and then communicated the knowledge of the event to the other. This would be a case of full information. To add realism to this example, consider Radner's (61) example. Decision maker I could be a production man and decision maker II a marketing man in the same company. The production man observes the event closest to him, the productivity of his department. The marketing man observes the event closest to him, the consumer demand. If each possesses full information, observes his event, and communicates it to the other, their joint decision of how much to produce to meet demand will be optimal.

The development of team decision theory has been primarily mathematical, but the basic notions have many behavioral implications, the main one being an indication of how communication affects human decision making. A more detailed look at communication structures will be found in the chapter on communication and structure. Whether decision making is approached by listing the procedures one goes through or by formulating a mathematical model, one point should be established by now: decision making is the choice among alternatives. A rational person would select the alternative which would maximize the desired result. But as Tannenbaum (72, p. 25) indicates, there are limits to rationality: a person does not know all alternatives present nor can he list all possible consequences. Simon (70, p. 62) has defined rationality in decision making as selecting the appropriate means for reaching the desired ends of the organization. But, "it is impossible for the behavior of a single, isolated individual to reach any high degree of rationality . . . the number of alternatives he must explore is so great, the information he would need to evaluate them so vast" (70, p. 79). As with the theory of teams example, a person acting without complete information is not able to make the optimal decision, or in Simon's terms, to choose that alternative which best leads to the organizational goal.

Since "rationality implies a complete, and unattainable, knowledge of the exact consequences of each choice" (70, p. 81), an organization usually becomes "concerned with the discovery and selection of satisfactory alternatives; only in exceptional cases is it concerned with the discovery and selection of optimal alternatives" (53, pp. 140–141). The organization is aware that it cannot expect optimal decisions; thus, it attempts to make them at least acceptable by imposing certain limits upon its members' decision-making behavior. The organization is so set up that in acting as a separate entity, it assigns a role to each decision maker, that is, "it specifies the particular values, facts, and alternatives upon which his decisions in the organization are to be based" (70, p. 198). Furthermore, the organization limits the types of decisions to be made by making the primary decisions. The "decisions which the organization makes for the individual ordinarily (1) specify . . . the general scope and nature of his duties; (2) allocate authority, that is, determine who in the organization is to have power to make further decisions . . . and (3) set other limits to his choice as are needed to coordinate the activities of several individuals in the organization" (70, pp. 8–9). The "organization" is merely a structure or a set of rules that have been developed by the organization's executives to reduce the decision-making duties to a manageable form.

Subordinates must usually accept the decisions of the organization even though they may be far from optimal. Tannenbaum (72, pp. 28–29) presents several reasons for the subordinates' accepting these decisions from their superiors. Since the superiors who make the decisions or pass them on are a source of authority, subordinates accept their decisions with some expectation that rewards, such as promotions, will follow such behavior. Then, too, the very act of accepting the decisions is perceived as being good for the company, since the decisions, by definition, were made to lead to coordination of tasks and organizational goal attainment. If the decisions passed on do all of this, then not accepting them would probably result in social disapproval from the subordinate's co-workers. The subordinate avoids accepting responsibility for a particular area when he accepts a decision from his superior. Of course, the acceptance of the superior's decision may be nothing more than respect for his age and experience in such matters.

March and Simon state that "the higher the organization level . . . the greater the felt need for joint decision making . . . because the rationale for the existence of a department lies largely in the need for coordination of its parts" (53, p. 124). The joint decision making allows just such coordination, especially in departments, where the greater the "mutual dependence on a limited resource, the greater the felt need for joint decision making with respect to that resource" (53, p. 122). It is not always true, though, that where joint decision making is called for it will be used effectively. Argyris (3) presents some evidence that because of certain personality problems, joint decision-making meetings do not always come up with better decisions. When rational approaches to a problem fail, emotional ones will be resorted to, with the entire decision-making atmosphere becoming emotional and personal rather than rational or logical. Argyris trained a group of top executives from a large national company in some of the principles he thought would create better inter-personal relationships and improve their decision-making effectiveness. Some of the principles he hoped to develop within them were: (1) "genu-ineness," accepting others without censure, being open to new ideas; (2) "descriptive non-evaluative feedback," telling others what effects a particu-lar action has on the group without introducing a value judgment of the member; (3) an awareness of their social impact upon others; and (4) a logical, rational response to the emotions of others rather than an emo-tional one. What he was developing was a free atmosphere for discussion and inquiry, "free" meaning not restricted by personality problems. Ap-parently, Argyris feels that through the training program the executives improved their decision-making environment, but no clear quantitative results are reported. The improvement, then, is in the relative ease in making decisions.

However, when their new-found approach to joint decision making was tried out on their subordinates, who had not been trained in these methods, more problems arose than were solved. The subordinates were highly suspicious of the increased freedom they were given in joint decision making with their superiors. It seems that what Argyris was trying to accomplish would work only if his "interpersonal principles" permeated the entire organization.

As in the case Argyris presents, Torrance says that in group decision making, "if the disagreements become centered in power roles and personalities, they are destructive . . . to . . . the group and its capability for productivity" (77, p. 318). But if the answers to the following ques-tions Torrance proposes are "yes," then the disagreements within the group are beneficial: "Does it [disagreement] increase the range of judg-ment? . . . Does it contribute to the elimination of misunderstanding? . . . Does it increase the group's ability to adapt? . . . Does it increase the group's willingness to take calculated risks in order to succeed?" (77, p. 318). Guetzkow and Gyr (33) have observed several business and govern-ment decision-making conferences to analyze disagreements and conflicts within them. They defined two types of conflict: (1) *substantive,* the ratio of the number of comments "opposing" the main issue to the total of "opposing" and "supporting" comments in the conference, and (2) *affective,* a measure of group frustration. They found that "groups in both types of conflict . . . tend not to terminate in consensus" (33, p. 372). (Consensus is the correspondence of individual opinion to group opinion and is measured by interviewing the conference participants at the end of the meeting.) When either type of conflict was present in a conference, "the relative absence of strong self-oriented needs increased the likelihood for consensus to appear" (p. 375). That is, when individuals who had a need for their own opinions to be heard and accepted were absent, group consensus was often achieved. Substantive conflict was usually reduced when facts were present and used and where efficient problem-solving procedures were used (p. 377). Affective conflict was not so easily re-moved but was somewhat eliminated when certain individuals causing group frustration withdrew from the conferences (p. 379). From a study of 108 company supervisors, Vroom (82, p. 324) concludes there is a significant positive relationship between participation in joint decision making and favorable attitudes toward the job, especially for those indi-viduals who have a high need for independence on the job. Joint decision making can be satisfying to the participants and can lead to better organiza-tional decisions but conflicts do arise in such situations; some ways of eliminating the conflict have been presented.

Maier and Solem (51) used 320 supervisors in groups of four each in a behavioral science laboratory to determine which of two solutions was better in a decision-making problem. The problem was a human relations one, involving resistance to a change of worker stations in a factory. The control group of supervisors were given several possible solutions to this artificial problem that was set up while the experimental group had to generate their own solution, i.e., they were given no solu-tions to choose from. It was found that the experimental groups made better decisions in each trial because the control groups merely selected an easy, obvious solution that was far from ideal. The implication is that in joint decision-making meetings, the generation of a solution to a problem (or a decision on a course of action) is superior to selecting a solution from a list of possible solutions drawn up by the head of the meeting. More work is involved in generating a solution, and findings indicate that it is precisely this extra effort that produces good solutions.

One study, at least, indicates that group decision making can be used to resolve a problem of fairness. Hoffman and Maier (39) used thirty groups, ranging in size from two to five college students, giving each group a relative number of grade points to distribute among its members; the experimenters wished to see how the groups would allocate these points among themselves. Of the 30 groups used, 23 allocated points among its members on the basis of need. That is to say, the lower the class standing of a person, as judged by previous exams in the course, the more points he received. Of course, those who received the points were pleased, but so too were those who gave "their" points away, for they had volunteered to do so without being pressured by the group. The authors suggest that such an approach might be used with a bonus plan in industry to see if the distribution here would occur on a need or an equal-share basis.

Supervisors are often called upon to make decisions about work rules violations, that is, they must decide what action to take on observing such violations. In a supervisory training program given in a large chemical company, Danielson and Maier (14) had first and second level supervisors engage in a role playing situation in order to come to a conclusion on a "best" way to handle the violation. The 308 supervisors were divided into groups of two, one "played" a supervisor, and the other, a repairman on a line. As the situation was set up, it *appeared* (but was not definitely known to the supervisor) that the repairman was not using his safety belt; the repairman was not sure whether his supervisor saw his safety belt unfastened. Some decision, on the part of the supervisor, had to be made; a penalty could be imposed or merely a reprimand or perhaps nothing. Seventy-five per cent of the supervisors discussed the violation with the repairmen, while the remaining did not and made a decision on the spot. Both approaches led to approximately the same number of repairmen indicating they would be more careful in the future. But those supervisors who discussed the violation, that is, tried to determine guilt or innocence, "motivated the repairman to lie, deny the violation, and in other situations where the repairman did admit the violation the foremen were put in a position of having to lay off the worker . . . and expose themselves to being accused of discriminating" (14, p. 169). The authors admit that in role playing, the people are not as emotionally involved as they would be if they were on the job but "the trends in results obtained with the use of this technique approximate those of the actual life situations" (p. 173). Further studies will have to be done before it is possible to say that the method discussed is the better approach in all similar situations.

Groups have been found to take greater risks than individuals would. Wallach, Kogan, and Bem (83) used fourteen groups of male students and fourteen groups of female students, with usually six persons per group, and had them consider hypothetical situations involving risk. Each situation had two alternatives, one a conservative one and the other a risky one, the latter having the greatest payoff attached. For example, "an electrical engineer may stick with his present job at a modest but adequate salary, or may take a new job offering considerably more money but no long-term security" (p. 77). Each person, alone, considered the situation and decided what odds he or she would take before advising the person to take the risky alternative. Then, this process was repeated by the group as a whole. For both sexes, there was "a strong move toward greater risk taking when groups arrive at unanimous decisions, compared with the risk levels ventured by the same persons in preddiscussion individual decisions" (83, p. 80). After the group decided, the individuals were again asked to indicate their odds and, now, the odds were on the side of risk-taking, presumably because of group discussions (p. 82). If the larger risk a group takes fails, each individual can blame the group, or other individuals, but in personal risk taking, there is no one with whom to share the blame. The "comfort" the group gives the individual helps to explain why groups do take larger risks in their decisions.

The leadership a group has can affect its risk-taking decisions as well as the quality of its decision making. Ziller (87) assigned 13 airplane crews to an authoritarian situation, 12 to a leader suggestion situation, 10 to a census situation, and 10 to a chairman situation. In the authoritarian situation, the leader made the decision with no discussion from the crew. In the leader suggestion situation, the leader stated his opinion, had a group discussion, then made the decision. For the census situation, there was first discussion, then the leader gave his opinion, a discussion followed, and then the leader made the decision. For the chairman situation, the group made the decision with the leader serving only as chairman of the discussion. Each crew was composed of about 10 to 11 men, and in all cases the leaders were the actual aircrew formal leaders. The decision related to a survival training problem, in which one of the alternatives was a risky one, possibly involving loss of life. Ziller found that "groups using leader-centered techniques of decision making (in which the leader has no knowledge of the group's opinion prior to stating his own opinion) are more reluctant than group-centered decision making groups to make a decision involving a risk of the lives of the group members" (pp. 387–388). The explanation, here, could be that groups prefer to decide their own fate rather than having it decided for them. Further comments on this are discussed in the chapter on group standards and pressure relating to notions of participative decision making.

It has been seen how the group atmosphere in decision making is affected by the leader; another important way it can be affected is by a certain understanding the group members can develop among themselves. A "brainstorming" atmosphere may also affect decision making favorably; in fact, this form of problem solving is frequently used when several solutions are desired. An atmosphere of creative thinking is developed by encouraging everyone in the group to propose solutions, no matter how wild they may be. The only rules are that there be no criticism of the ideas, and the more ideas the better. It had been thought that groups in a brainstorming atmosphere would produce better solutions than individuals working alone, but research indicates this is not so. Taylor, Berry, and Block (75) compared 48 college students working alone on three different qualitative problems requiring creative solutions with 12 groups of 4 students each working on the same problems. All the students were briefed on the so-called rules of brainstorming and asked to proceed accordingly on the problems given them. The groups of four were called the *real* groups. After the individuals each attempted the problems, they were randomly divided into groups of four—these were the *nominal* groups. The results of the real groups were then compared to the results of the nominal groups, the sum of the individual scores in it. The nominal groups, i.e., the individuals, produced more solutions, more feasible and unique ones than the real groups. "Performance of the real groups is inferior to that of the nominal groups on all three problems with respect to each and all of the measures of performance employed" (p. 43). Taylor, *et al.* suggest that a common approach tends to develop in the real groups, from which individuals find it difficult to deviate. The justification for comparing the real groups with the nominal groups is that both involve the same number of man-minutes in the problem solution (real groups have 4 members working for a total of 12 minutes giving 48 man-minutes and the nominal groups are composed of 4 members each of whom worked alone for 12 minutes giving 48 man-minutes also), but the first is a group of 4 working together and the latter is the sum of 4 individuals working alone. The results indicate whether individuals working together are better or worse than individuals working alone.

A replication, or equivalent repetition, of this experiment was done by Dunnette, Campbell, and Jaastad (18) on some employees of the Minnesota Mining and Manufacturing Company, and similar results were found. The subjects in this experiment worked both in nominal and real groups. The real groups were composed for the most part of men who had worked together in the past and of men with the same status so that no one assumed authority over the others, thereby destroying the "creative" atmosphere. Twelve groups of 4 research scientists were involved in the study and "only 5 of the 48 research subjects failed to produce more ideas when working individually than when participating in a group" (p. 34). An addition of 12 groups of four advertising personnel each gave cumulative results of 23, out of the total 24, groups producing more individually than collectively. By using the same subjects in both the real and nominal groups, the effects of practice could be ascertained, as one-half the subjects would start in the nominal groups and finish in the real groups, and the other half would start in the real groups and finish in the nominal groups. It was found that when individual brainstorming followed group brainstorming more ideas were produced than when it preceded group brainstorming; as the authors suggest, the group approach could be a "warm-up" for individual efforts.

As pointed out, the brainstorming approach requires a particular atmosphere that lends itself to creative problem solving. Some conditions leading to creative problem solving have been proposed by Hoffman (37). His Condition 1 is: "Differing, but comparable cognitions must coexist" (p. 430). Each person in the problem-solving group must have an opportunity to suggest alternatives and to play a creative role in the decision-making process. His Condition 2 is "At least two differing cognitions must acquire greater positive valence [attractiveness] than the minimum threshold value . . . and must be approximately equal in value, so that none of the alternatives can be accepted and an impasse is reached" (p. 434). This means there must be at least two different approaches, of about the same quality, that are more attractive than some predetermined minimum standard of attractiveness. If at least two equally attractive alternatives exist, "the creative solution to such a problem would exploit the advantages of both alternatives and minimize the disadvantages" (p. 434). Condition 3 is: "Problem solving must occur in a situation in which the problem-solving unit is required to arrive at the best possible decision" (p. 435). A search for the best solution should assure a greater effort or motivation to develop creative solutions. A less important condition is his Condition 4, "The cognitive components of the valence of each of the conflicting alternatives should be abstracted and their points of conflict recognized" (p. 437). In other words, there should be an awareness of the conflict different alternatives present so that points of conflict can be resolved and the creative solution formulated. Hoffman's conditions merely say that the necessary conditions for creative problem solving are to have a problem that can be "attacked" many different ways and to recognize this when developing a final solution.

The personality homogeneity, or lack of it, of the members in a group also can be thought of as relating to the group atmosphere. Hoffman and Maier (40) formed 16 homogeneous and 25 heterogeneous groups of four college students each. Those in the homogeneous groups were said to have similar, and those in the heterogeneous groups quite different, personalities as judged by their "scores" on certain personality tests. All the groups had to solve five problems in the human relations field. For the problems, "the solutions by heterogeneous groups either were scored as significantly superior in quality to those of the homogeneous groups, or did not differ in quality" (p. 402). The authors suggest that the similar personalities of the homogeneous groups led to similar insights and perspectives, while for the heterogeneous groups, "the conflict resulting from opposing viewpoints may have caused more complete solutions to emerge or new ones to be invented" (p. 406). Kelly and Thibaut (42, p. 771) also indicate that group homogeneity may reduce the problem-solving effectiveness of a group.

Little mention is ever made in decision making of the probability of a particular person making a series of correct decisions just by chance alone. However, Deutsch and Madow (16) have presented an explanation of why chance favors a certain individual in making a series of correct decisions. To demonstrate, four quantities must be defined: $m, y, p,$ and n. Let $m =$ the number of decision makers involved in making the same general decisions; $y =$ the expected number of decision makers who will make the series of correct decisions; $p =$ the probability of making a correct decision each time a decision is made; $n =$ the number of correct decisions in a series that are made. Using an example of Deutsch and Madow's (p. 74), if $p = \frac{2}{3}$, $n = 4$, and $y = 1$, then $m = 5$. This means if there are five decision makers (m) involved in making decisions about the same kind of things, and if a series of four decisions (n) are made, with a probability of $\frac{2}{3}$ (p) that each decision made will be correct, then one person (y) can be expected to make all four decisions correctly by chance alone. The formula which expresses this relationship is

$$m = y\,(1/p)^n.$$

Put another way, if the probability of making eight correct decisions in a row is, say, 1/256, then one person out of 256 persons will be expected to make all eight decisions correctly because of chance. The obvious implication is that not all those individuals in an organization who are considered to be excellent decision makers are necessarily excellent decision makers. The problem, then, is to separate the chaff from the wheat.

Some findings about decision making in organizations and groups have been presented, and, while it is difficult to formulate a brief conclusion for the many diverse studies reported on, one general conclusion can be made about managerial decision making in the future. Studies, such as those by Mann and Williams (52), indicate that as a company changes over to electronic data processing, certain decision-making levels in the company will either vanish or become less important. In the utility company that Mann and Williams observed, "the level of decision making and control . . . moved up to fewer and higher positions within the organization (52, p. 255). The data processing equipment essentially serves as a decision maker on one of the levels within an organization. The implications for organizational behavior are at least two. First, there will be resistance to this change; second, structural changes in the organization will be necessary, involving retraining of personnel, dislocation, and the like.

Problem Solving

Reviews of the literature of problem solving have been done by Kelly and Thibaut (42), Taylor and McNemar (74), Gagne (31) and Duncan (17). These reviews cover a larger area of problem solving than this section will and should be consulted if depth into theories of thinking and concept formation is desired. As mentioned in the introduction to this chapter, problem solving here will emphasize those findings which can be easily related to behavior in organizations; it will not discuss the complex psychological theories underlying the more theoretical aspects of problem solving. While the previous section focused on finding *a* solution to the problem, assuming that there was no predetermined "correct" solution, this section will focus on finding the solution, i.e., the objectively correct one. However, since the distinction between the two, decision making and problem solving, is not always neat, there will be some overlap. For instance, in relating communication nets to problem solving, some of the researchers use "human relations" problems, which do not have correct solutions, and others use a task of logic, which does have a correct solution.

"Problem solving in human adults is a name for a diverse class of performances which differs, if it differs at all, only in degree from other classes of learning and performance, the degree of difference depending upon the extent to which problem solving demands location or integration of previously learned responses" (17, p. 425). Thinking generally involves the integration of past experiences, while problem solving adds to this, as Duncan (17, p. 397) has pointed out, "the dimension of discovery." Thus, "problem solving occurs when the individual cannot reach that goal by means of behavior based simply on reflexes or habits" (31, p. 147). What are sought, then, are the correct responses which, taken in the proper sequence, will lead to *the* solution of the problem. There may be several solutions or approaches to the problem as in intra-organizational decision making but, unlike that type of decision making, the correct answer will be known when it is found—because there is only one answer.

Merrifield, Guilford, Christensen, and Frick (56) have investigated the intellectual factors used in problem solving to discover what dimensions of intellect appear relevant to problem-solving behavior. For a large variety of problems, they found the following significant dimensions or factors by using factor analysis (pp. 3–4): verbal comprehension, conceptual foresight, originality, and sensitivity to the problems. The first factor implies an "awareness of the meanings of words or ideas" so that the problem is thoroughly understood in the light of proposed solutions. Conceptual foresight is an *awareness of* "antecedents, concurrents, or consequents of given information" so that the information can be properly used. Originality is the "production of a variety of changes of interpretation, neither immediate nor obvious, that are appropriate" to the problem's solution. Sensitivity to the problem involves the *evaluation* of the "antecedents, concurrents, or consequents of given information." It would be expected that people possessing these four problem-solving factors could do a better job of problem solving than others not possessing them, other things being equal.

Once a group begins the problem-solving process, they should, according to Bales and Strodtbeck (5), "tend to move in their interaction from a relative emphasis upon problems of *orientation,* to problems of *evaluation,* and subsequently to problems of *control*" (p. 625), and the number of negative and positive behaviors in the group should increase. This is known as the "phase hypothesis." In studying several laboratory groups engaging in many problem-solving activities, they found most of the groups initially concerned themselves with giving and asking for orientation, that is, clarifying and confirming information needed for the solution. The evaluation phase consists of giving and asking of opinions and feelings about the problem under discussion. Finally, the control phase develops as suggestions and directions for action are given. As the group life ages, there appears to be a greater amount of emotional reactions occurring in the form of disagreements or agreements, antagonism or solidarity, tension or tension release. This determination of group behavior was made through the use of an interaction scoring system called Interaction Process Analysis, developed by Bales. While the group is in session, trained observers check off on a list the interaction activities of the group members. Such a list is presented in Figure 2. According to the phase hypothesis, problem-solving groups should, as time progresses, exhibit behavior falling more in the control categories and negative and positive reactions as judged by the observers. These results are expected on problems having some uncertainty of facts, where judgment is necessary and where there is some pressure for a group solution.

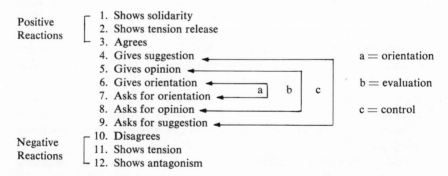

Figure 2. Interaction process analysis scheme. (From Robert F. Bales and Fred L. Strodtbeck, Phases in Group Problem Solving, *Journal of Abnormal and Social Psychology,* 1951, 46, 485–495. Reprinted with permission of the American Psychological Association and the senior author.)

While some pressure developed within a group is necessary for effective problem solving, pressure that becomes stressful can produce restraining effects. Cowen (12) has shown what effects psychological stress has upon problem-solving behavior. He used two sets of groups of undergraduates solving the "water-jar problem" (where there are, say, three water-jars each holding a different amount of water and the problem is to come up with an amount of water that can only be obtained by taking certain combinations of the three given water-jars). One set of groups, the control, solved the water-jar problems under an informal and casual atmosphere, and the other set, the experimental groups, solved the problems in a formal and business-like atmosphere. Both groups were given the same set of problems, which were so arranged that the first ones could be solved by the application of one rule the group could induce from its early results. One of the final problems, however, was of such a nature that it required an entirely new rule of solution, i.e., the previous method would no longer work. The stress groups experienced not only a formal atmosphere but also individual criticism—the pressure was both organizational and personal. It was found that the stress groups more often continued to work the new problem by the old method (the old rule) than did the control groups, which usually sought a new approach to the problem. The stress groups were probably more rigid in their problem-solving behavior because they were searching for security against the perceived threat of pressure by following "safe" behavior. Their search for security was an attempt, conscious or not, to combat stress.

Another experiment involving stress was conducted by Anderson (2) using 48 Navy enlisted men solving problems in the calculus of propositions, where specific conclusions are to be drawn from certain given premises. Depending on the situation, the men were given either one, two, three or four conclusions to reach from the given premises; in all the multiple-goal cases, the problem was considered solved when the one proper conclusion was reached. The results indicated the "number of solutions is an inverse function of number of goals" (p. 303)—the more goals to be solved, the fewer the number of correct solutions. The goals to be reached interfered with each other; since only one of the goals, or conclusions, was obtainable, attempts to reach the other ones were a waste of time.

Further examples of problem solving under stress come under the heading of individual performance in front of an audience. "We are fairly certain that simple tasks are performed more rapidly when spectators are present than when the subject is alone" (53, p. 103), though, as Kelly and Thibaut (42, p. 750) point out, the greater output of work applies only to physical work, not work involving mental concentration. In the first instance, the audience increases the subject's motivation to work harder, but in the latter instance, "social stimuli are able to compete successfully with the task stimuli" (42, p. 750). There is some indication, however, "that these effects wear off as the person adapts to the social situation" (42, p. 750). Wapner and Alper (84) used 120 subjects to solve word problems in three conditions: alone with the experimenter, alone with the experimenter plus an unseen audience, and alone with the experimenter plus a seen audience. The condition of working just with the experimenter produced the greatest output, and the condition of working with the experimenter and the unseen audience produced the least output. The anxiety of working before an unseen audience appears to be greater than that before a seen audience, since when the unseen is speculated about, apprehension usually results.

All this is not to say that stress or anxiety is always harmful to a group or individual problem-solving performance. Rather, a certain tension level is necessary for optimal performance; too little tension is a sign of too little motivation and too much tension is a sign of reduced flexibility. Van Buskirk (80) used undergraduates to solve logical deduction problems from a list of given propositions, and on the basis of their scores on an anxiety test, divided them into low and high anxiety groups. He found the high anxiety did better on the problems than the low anxiety groups. His explanation was that the high anxiety person "is more strongly committed to performing well as long as the experimental situation does not present a serious, ego-involving threat" (p. 208). The necessary motivational level for good performance was reached only by those in the "high anxiety" category; but should an ego threat develop, it would be expected that this category would have reduced problem-solving flexibility in accordance with the increased tension. The terms "stress," "anxiety," and "tension" have been used synonymously here; although they are somewhat different, gross interpretation errors will not result in this discussion if they are used interchangeably.

The communication structure the group operates in has an effect on problem-solving efficiency as Bavelas (7) has shown. A full discussion of communication and group structure will be found in the chapter of the same name, but two studies by Shaw, et al. (65, 68) have a direct bearing on problem-solving efficiency and can also serve as an introduction to communication nets. One study by Shaw (65) used 24 groups of 3 male college students problem solving in a Wheel and Circle communication network. These communication networks can be found with some other networks in Figure 3. (The dots indicate individuals in the network and the lines connecting them indicate the communication channels. If there is no line connecting individuals, then they do not communicate.) The problems they had to solve consisted of a simple word problem and a complex arithmetic problem both of which were to be solved by the three-man group as a whole, using both communication nets and sending written messages along the channels. The results indicated that "with complex

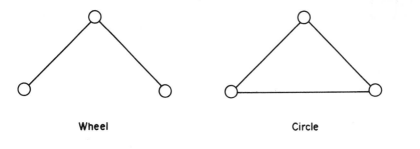

Wheel   Circle

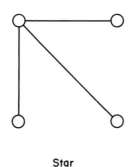

Star

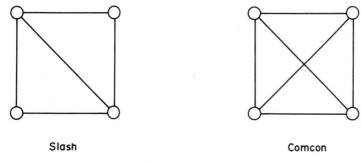

Slash   Comcon

Figure 3. Some communication networks used in problem-solving experiments.

problems, the circle is faster than the wheel . . . with simple problems, the wheel is faster than the circle" (p. 213). As Shaw explains, on a simple problem to solve, each person is willing to accept the word or decision of any other person in the net and complete communication among all members is not necessary. In fact, on a simple problem, complete communication (as in the circle network) slows down the problem-solving process; hence, the wheel network is faster. But for a complex problem, complete communication among members is necessary, and the circle network allows for faster complete communication than the wheel network. Another group of male undergraduates was used by Shaw, Rothschild, and Strickland (68) to solve human relations problems in three different communication nets, the Star, Slash, and Comcon types, as depicted in Figure 3. As before, each group of four had to come to a group solution by passing written communications back and forth according to the net structure. It was found that the "time required to reach a decision was longest in the star and shortest in the comcon" (p. 325). The number of communications needed to make a good decision in each of the nets was about the same, but in the Comcon net, the speed in which the communications were sent was faster than the others. Assuming the human relations problems were complex, then by Shaw's first experiment, the results could be explained by saying complete communication among members is necessary—and this the Comcon net achieves most quickly. Were the human relations problems simple, complete communication would not be necessary and the Comcon net should no longer be the best one.

There are many ways in which to study problem-solving behavior depending on the experimental design used. A taxonomy of commonly used designs or approaches has been drawn up by Lorge, Fox, Davitz and Brenner (46, p. 340). The three main classifications are: (1) "Interacting, face-to-face group, i.e., involving group meeting and discussion"; (2) "Noninteracting face-to-face group, i.e., involving physical meeting, but no discussion"; (3) "Noninteracting non-face-to-face group, i.e., involving no meeting and no discussion." Classification (1) is the "typical" group meeting where everyone interacts with one another. These groups may be *ad hoc,* existing for the experiment only, or *traditioned,* real-life groups having a history of previous existence. An example of this classification is a study by Taylor and Faust (73). Classification (2) can be divided into those situations where either there is a measure of the group opinion by, say, the total show of hands or there is a measure of an individual's opinion as a result of his being in the presence of others. An example of this classification is a study by Barnlund (6). Classification (3) is really an artifact because the measure of "group" performance here is either measured by averaging individual performances and calling the result for these individuals the "group" performance or measured by combining in another way, such as summing individual performances and calling this the "group" product. An example of this classification is a study by Faust (28).

Group problem-solving "refers to the psychological and social processes whereby individual solutions are created, communicated, and eventually assembled into a product that represents the group" (42, p. 738). Any group member's motivation to work on the group task can depend upon "the degree of identification with the group, the amount of responsibility felt for the outcome of the problem-solving process, and the kinds of rewards given for successful task completion" (42, p. 743). If an individual perceives himself as being a part of the group, responsible for helping the group reach a solution, and is satisfied with the rewards, material or otherwise, he will receive if the solution is reached, chances are he will be motivated to help achieve the group goal. Given that all or most of the group members are so motivated, then it would be expected that because of the group interaction, the group's product would differ from any individual's. Because of the pooling of individual judgments in a group, the group should be superior, in at least one respect, over an individual in problem solving, simply because the group outnumbers the individual. In problems involving large amounts of information to be handled, one or two individuals may not be able to handle it all while a group could; hence, this is one respect in which a group could be superior to an individual. But is the group superior to individuals working alone in all cases? "Any generalization that groups are superior to individuals on problem-solving tasks must be extremely tentative at best" (8, p. 170) conclude Brim, et al., after a review of the literature.

One of the early experiments comparing group solutions with individual ones was done in 1932 by Shaw (69). She used groups of four college students each; the groups were required to solve the complex problems involving a number of steps that had to be correct before the final answer emerged. Individuals working alone also solved the same problems. The groups solved more problems accurately than did the individuals, if for no other reason than a group of four has three more people working on a problem than an individual does. A more specific explanation of the results can be attributed to an "error-correcting mechanism" operating within a group. The steps necessary to reach a solution, though perhaps formulated by one individual, are considered and evaluated by the group as a whole and errors generated in the solution are usually caught in the evaluation process. Barnlund states that because of the error-correcting mechanism, "errors that might have been committed privately were checked before they were communicated to others" (6, p. 58). He formed small groups of college students so that individuals within each group had about the same problem-solving ability (as judged by tests). Ability was distributed equally within groups so as to reduce any effects the factor of "distributed ability" may have had on the solutions. The groups mentioned, plus individuals working alone, solved problems in logic. Problems were solved both by a majority rule of the group members, that is with no group interaction, and by the usual interaction method. "Majority rule, when it precludes discussion or debate, is likely to be less effective than the personal judgment of superior members of the group" (6, p. 58). But, "after discussion . . . groups produced decisions that were far superior to those of members working alone" (p. 58). Similar results were found by Gurnee (34).

Gurnee had five different groups, ranging in size from 18 to 66 subjects, take three different true or false tests on an individual basis. Then each group as a whole was asked to take the tests by a show of hands. It was found the group scores were higher than the average of the individual scores in a group. Of course, it is possible that, since the group solutions were subsequent to the individual ones, the groups had the advantage of having already "solved" the problems as individuals. Thus, the groups had more time to think about the problems than the individuals did. Contrary to Barnlund's (6) experiment, there was no group discussion; thus the result of each person's voting by raising his hand in his group could be influenced by the other group members. While there was no direct interaction, there was indirect interaction as Gurnee stated that "doubtful subjects would often tend to delay their . . . reactions just long enough to observe the dominant side, then would vote accordingly" (34, p. 110). He also found, as did Barnlund, that the group was seldom superior to the best individual in it, since three of his five groups did worse than the best individuals in them.

Other studies (28, 35, 41, 45, 53, 73) also have indicated, for one reason or another, group superiority over individuals in problem solving. Taylor and Faust (73) used 105 college students divided randomly into groups of two and four, as well as individuals working alone. They were to play "Twenty Questions," guessing a subject, given it was either animal, vegetable or mineral, in twenty questions that could be answered by either "yes" or "no." Actually thirty questions were needed rather than twenty. It was found "group performances were superior to individual performance in terms of number of questions, number of failures, and elapsed time per problem" (p. 365). Husband (41) used college students, some working as individuals and some in groups of two, to solve arithmetic problems and found the groups took less time to solve the problems. Lorge, *et al.* (45) used teams of five Air Force R.O.T.C. students and individuals working alone to solve a military problem of getting a squad of soldiers across a mined road as quickly and secretly as possible. The problem was solved at four differing degrees of reality ranging from a verbal description of the situation to a model of the situation where miniature soldiers could be manipulated by hand. The groups and individuals could ask the experimenters as many questions as they wished in solving the problems.

For all degrees of reality, the groups gave better solutions than the individuals. However, as the authors point out, since the groups asked more questions, they obtained more information and this may account for the groups' superiority.

It was mentioned before that a group could, in many cases, do better than individuals because of more manpower at its disposal. The question of motivation also enters in. Lorge, Fox, Davitz, and Brenner (46, pp. 341–342) suggest that the motivation of an individual working alone may be low, while in a group one person's low motivation is not likely to affect the total performance. Furthermore, "participation in groups may be important because it motivates individuals in situations in which motivation may otherwise be inadequate" (28, p. 71). To offset the effects of pooling, scores of nominal groups are compared with those of real groups; that is, the group score of n individuals working together has to be compared with the average or total score of n individuals working alone. With this comparison, groups no longer have a pooling advantage and if groups still prove superior, it is now for other reasons.

Marquart (54) compared college students working alone with students in groups of three (usually consisting of two men and one woman) in solving several problems requiring creative thought. "If one considers the ratio of the number of solutions obtained to the number of possible solutions, the group solved many more problems than did the individuals" (p. 109). For one set of problems, the "average time required for correct solutions by the groups working as groups is slightly higher than the average time required for the groups working as individuals" (p. 110), but for another set of problems the reverse was true because of the difficulty individuals working alone had with the particular problem. Normally individuals are somewhat more efficient, time wise, in problem solving. Using 236 undergraduates either working alone or in groups of four, Faust (28) gave them a verbal and a spatial problem to solve. "On spatial problems, group performance was significantly superior to individual performance . . . on verbal problems, group performance was also superior to individual performance" (p. 71). When nominal groups were compared to real groups, there was no significant difference between them on the spatial problems and essentially none for the verbal problems. Hall, Mouton, and Blake (35) had industrial managers taking part in a human relations training program make judgments, as individuals and as groups, as to the outcome of a human relations situation. The groups, in size from 6 to 8 people, were to interact and come up with a unanimous decision. The results "demonstrate that group effort produced a more accurate score than the average of pooled individual scores" (p. 152). It appears that interaction, more than pooling, accounts for the group's superiority.

Hall, Mouton, and Blake (35) also found that for 17 of the 22 groups they used, "the highest individual prediction was superior or equal to the group prediction" (p. 152). Taken along with the previously mentioned results of Barnlund (6), and Gurnee (34), the conclusion is that a superior individual will usually do better at a problem-solving task than any group will. As has been said, "A committee did not write *Hamlet*." Where coordination among the group members is needed for problem solution, individuals working alone prove superior, as McCurdy and Lambert (50) have pointed out. In another problem given to graduate students, Lorge and Solomon (47) found "where individuals and members of the group do not report familiarity with the problem, the proportion of correct solutions decreases as size of group is larger" (p. 113). The problem involved coordination of activities, i.e., of thoughts; the more people involved in it, the more time spent in *coordinating* the activities and the less time spent in actually *solving* the problem. Porter (60) gave individuals and groups of two, four, and eight a difficult problem to solve where each person had only $1/n$, where n equals the size of the group, of the necessary information to solve the problem. Thus an individual working alone had $1/1$ or all the information; in a group of four, each person had $\frac{1}{4}$ of the information, and so on. Each group, therefore, had complete information. The individuals solved the problem 13% of the time as compared to the best group (composed of four members) which solved the problem 4% of the time. The groups required coordination within them to distribute the information among all the members. Alternatively, when each person in the groups possessed *all* the information, as the group size increased, the percentage of correct solutions also increased (except for a group of size two where the interactions between members interrupted their problem solving) as coordination of information was not necessary. Actually, most problem-solving tasks given to groups involve some degree of coordination of activities, but this is not to say that individuals will always do better than groups. Only where coordination is a major part of the problem-solving process does it affect the process; otherwise, the coordination difficulties are easily overcome and the pooling and interaction effects become dominant.

Individuals surpass groups in problems involving coordination and also in efficiency of problem solving. Husband (41) found that individuals needed less man-minutes to solve arithmetic problems than did groups. Man-minutes as a measure of efficiency is the product of the number of persons working on the problem multiplied by the time spent on the problem. For example, four people working on a problem for five minutes (4×5) is equivalent to one person working on the problem for twenty minutes (1×20). Taylor and Faust (73) also found individuals more efficient according to this criterion, as have several other researchers. In fact, Duncan (17) after reviewing the literature states, "where efficiency measures were reported, and also probably where they were not reported, individuals were superior" (p. 418). To say groups are better than individuals or that individuals are better than groups at problem solving requires a definition of "better." Individuals are better when coordination problems are severe, when efficiency is a criterion, and when a brainstorming atmosphere is being used, pooling effects held constant; otherwise groups are "better."

There has been some concern in determining what size group is "best" for problem-solving tasks in terms of obtaining the solution the soonest, but it is not possible to state definitively that a group of size n is the best for all situations. To do so requires finding an optimum group size and then proving it to be optimum—no such techniques exist in the social sciences. However, the indication is that a group size of 5 or 7 is better than most size groups. Ziller (88) used fifty groups of Air Force bomber crews of sizes 2, 3, 4, 5, and 6 members. They were all given a problem and fifteen facts relevant to solving it; it was their job to choose the most important four facts bearing on the problem. The group of size 6 did the best but since there were no larger groups, it is not possible to say size 6 was better than a larger group. Slater (71) used undergraduates of sizes of 2, 3, 4, 5, 6, and 7 members discussing a human relations problem. The members in each group were asked whether they thought their group was too small or too large for the problem at hand. For the group of 5, none of the members felt it was too large or too small, while no one felt either that groups of 2, 3, 4 were too large or that groups of 6, 7 were too small. "Members of larger groups feel that the group is disorderly and wastes time . . . [such groups] produced more difficulties in communication, and inhibited individual participation" (p. 134). For the smaller groups, there was a fear of alienation if ideas were freely expressed that in a larger group would be taken as less personal. Hare (36, pp. 243–244) feels that a group of five is near optimal and possesses three positive characteristics. First with an odd number in the group, no deadlock is possible. Second, being in the minority does not isolate the person as a deviant as it might in a group of, say, three. Third, "the group appears to be large enough for the members to shift roles easily" for a proper allocation of tasks (the various roles existing in a group are mentioned in the chapter on leadership). The trend toward an optimal size of about five or seven is clear, but the "proof" is lacking.

Individual Choice Behavior

Individual choice behavior falls into two categories: it may be either decision making when the problem does not have one best choice (alternative), or problem solving when there is a definite best choice. Decision making is the larger category because decisions, right or wrong, must always be made about something. And decision usually involves risk-taking, for example, in gambling, deciding what to bet upon and how much to bet. While most of the experiments have simulated betting situations, the attempt has basically been to understand risk-taking behavior of all kinds: in business, the military, in gambling, etc. The discovery of an adequate mathematical model, a representation of reality, would allow the prediction in a mathematically accurate sense of choices people make. So far several models account for small aspects of choice behavior, but no one model yet exists that accurately coordinates them. This section will present only a brief introduction to individual choice behavior and some simple mathematical models; a book by Luce (48) and one by Luce and Raiffa (49) and a review article by Edwards (25) go into the area much more deeply.

There has been criticism directed at the mathematical approaches to decision making on an individual choice behavior level because of the apparent narrowness. A typical criticism is one by Gagne who states the mathematical approaches "(a) utilize assumptions about human decision making which go far beyond what is known about such behavior; and (b) require the construction of highly specialized situations as tests of model predictions" (31, p. 167). Not all models define away some of the less understood decision-making processes, but most do test their models in highly specialized situations. A possible advantage of such research, though, is the discovery of "universals" of decision-making behavior that, in time, may be applied to all types of activities.

In choosing among alternatives, an individual in some way sets up a scale to weigh and order them; this usually unconscious evaluation enables him to make the choices. Certain events in the real world come with numbers attached—others do not. To choose between earning one dollar and two dollars for the same amount of work presents no problem. But to make a decision as to which of several persons should be promoted is not so clear; numbers for all of the comparisons are not available. Yet, people do make decisions like this and many are good decisions. The important thing is to evaluate each of the alternatives and to choose the alternatives having the highest value—in other words to maximize the value of the choice. As Edwards has said, "people behave as if they were attempting to maximize some quantity—perhaps not skillfully, perhaps not consistently, but still attempting to maximize" (24, p. 110).

Mathematically, the expected value (EV) of an event or series of events can easily be defined as the product of the probability of the event occurring (p) times the value (V) or payoff the event will have for the person, summed over all the events i. That is, $EV = \sum_i p_i V_i$.

For instance, if a person holds one of ten tickets to a lottery that will pay the winner \$20, the $EV = (1/10)$ \$20 $=$ \$2. This simple model could be used as a predictor of individual choice behavior by assuming the individual was attempting to maximize the EV of the choice-alternatives present. He would in some way compute the EV for each of the alternatives and choose that alternative having the largest EV. But studies of gambling situations, where EV's can easily be computed, have shown that individuals do not always maximize the EV. Apparently, they only choose acceptable alternatives and not the best ones. "People in gambling situations do not make choices in such a way as to maximize their expected earnings or minimize their expected losses" (19, p. 349). Edwards has performed several experiments where subjects were given the opportunity of choosing gambling bets having many different EV's. The results of one experiment by him indicate that individuals "do not consistently prefer bets with higher EV's to bets with lower EV's" (20, p. 66). Another experiment by Coombs and Komorita shows "that people have definite preferences among bets with equal expected monetary value" (10, p. 389). Furthermore, the mere fact that people gamble when the odds are against them, i.e., the EV's are negative, indicates there is no desire to maximize EV.

Any expected value is a function of two variables: the probability p and the value V. Rather than maximizing both of them, i.e., the EV, only one, p, is usually maximized. A study by Edwards (21) points up the fact that most of the subjects showed probability preferences rather than money value preferences; there was an attempt at p rather than EV maximization. It is not unreasonable to assume a person will choose a p of .9 and a V of 100 ($EV = 90$) over a p of .4 and a V of 300 ($EV = 120$) if the person is more concerned with winning something, because of the higher probability, than with winning nothing. If such results can be generalized, it could be said that a manager making a business decision, involving risk, would not choose the alternative maximizing the expected value of the return to the company, but the one with the greatest probability of a success, i.e., the safest alternative. This may be typical behavior in large conservative organizations but certainly does not hold for entrepreneurs.

Thus far, the discussion has made no reference to the utility or usefulness of the possible payoffs. In fact, the value or payoff (V) has no such applicability, since it is a given value in the situation and in itself tells nothing of its usefulness to the decision makers. Values and utilities are not the same, then. Say that a man in a business needs \$300 to close an important transaction and he has *only* two quick investment alternatives to choose from to obtain this amount. One alternative has a $p = .9$ of earning \$100 (V) and the other alternative has a $p = .4$

of earning \$300 (*V*). He would not make a choice on the basis of maximizing the *EV*'s, as neither alternative has an *EV* equal to or greater than the \$300 he needs. He would not make a selection on the basis of maximizing *p*, as the alternative with the highest *p* would only gain him \$90 and he needs \$300. Obviously, he would make his choice on the basis of value—on which alternative provides the necessary \$300. Actually the notion of utility is the basis on which his choice is made, because he is concerned not with the value per se, but with the usefulness or utility of it. In this case, value and utility overlap, but usually utility is an approach to value when dollar values are not present, that is, when clear-cut numerical values for comparison are not at hand. When an event does not possess *inherent* numerical values, it is proper to speak of the event as having a utility rather than a value. Numbers may be attached to the event, however, so that utilities can be compared, but these are approximations. Where a utility (*U*) is used in place of a value (*V*), the *EV* now becomes *EU*, expected utility; thus, $EU = \sum_i p_i U_i$.

An individual cannot as readily compare assigned numbers of utilities as he can dollar values. People cannot "discriminate perfectly between alternatives with respect to preferences" (49, p. 373), and can do little more than rank utility preferences, stating in which order the utilities of various alternatives are preferred. The fact of the matter is, an individual "does not measure his utilities exactly but rather conducts his economic activities in a sphere of considerable haziness" (81, p. 20). With regard to the *EU* model, Mosteller and Nogee stated in 1951, "the notion that people behave in such a way as to maximize their expected utility is not unreasonable" (58, p. 403). And it is not unreasonable that individuals would choose that alternative having the highest expected usefulness to them. Previous to this, Von Neumann and Morgenstern (81) "defended this model and, thus, made it apparent, but in 1954 it was already clear that it too does not fit the facts" (25, p. 474). Instead of maximizing *EU*, most people seem to make decisions on the basis of the utilities of the various alternatives but do not combine them with the probabilities of occurrence.

The probabilities dealt with are known as objective probabilities because they represent reality, or nature, as it is and are not subject to interpretation. In flipping a fair coin, the probability of getting "heads" is ½; this is not a guess or an estimate of the outcome, but indicates the outcome as represented by nature. There are such things as subjective probabilities, however, which are estimates of objective probabilities. These subjective probabilities are to objective ones as utilities are to values. Where the numerical values are not present, utilities are formed; where objective probabilities are not present, subjective ones are formed. For example, a businessman is considering several locations on which to build a plant. He does not know exactly what monetary return or value each location would give him so he must assign a utility or usefulness measure to each location. Thus, each plant location will have a utility, an estimate of an objective value, attached to it by the decision maker. There is no objective probability available to indicate his "chances" of each utility being realized so he must estimate with subjective probabilities.

In gambling experiments where objective probabilities are known for the outcomes of dice, card games, roulette, etc., people ignore them and formulate their own subjective probabilities. Even where a series of events is independent, as in a series of coin tosses, there is a tendency "to predict the outcome which has occurred less frequently in the past" (9, p. 37). If the past five flips of a coin have yielded five "heads," a person would not accept the objective probability of .5 of another "heads" occurring and would assign a subjective probability of less than .5 that another "heads" would occur. As Alberoni (1, p. 262) points out, subjects assume a phenomenon is due to chance (such as when "heads" appear most of the time); in seeking to explain it they resort to subjective probabilities. At first thought, it appears the subjects are naïve with respect to the objective probabilities that exist. But an experiment by Scodel, Ratoosh, and Minas indicated "people who are very much aware of objective probabilities and expected return are governed by other considerations in their risk-taking preferences" (64, p. 26). Littig has "hypothesized that lower objective probabilities of success would be preferred by subjects who believed that they could use skill to influence outcome than by subjects who believed outcome was a matter of chance alone" (44, p. 67). In making decisions, people do not always believe the objective probabilities they know to be correct.

If for the EV model, subjective probability is substituted for objective probability, we will have a subjectively expected value model. (SEV) defined as $SEV = \sum_i \psi_i V_i$ where ψ is the subjective probability. However, "no one since 1954 has defended the subjective probability-objective value model" (25, p. 475) as a model for decision making. When both utility and subjective probability notions are combined, we have the subjectively expected utility model (SEU) of decision making (23, 24). For similar gambling experiments, as used in the other models, Edwards has found that individuals "choose the bet with the maximum subjectively expected utility" (23, p. 214). For a more general decision-making situation, Brim, *et al.,* found that "both mothers and fathers selected among child-rearing alternatives as if they were maximizing their [subjectively] expected utilities" (8, p. 216). Among the four different models presented (EV, EU, SEV, SEU), it appears the SEU one has the most promise in predicting which alternative a person will choose in gambling situations. A generalization of the results, though, remains somewhat tentative.

Personality factors also relate to how people make decisions. Scodel,

Ratoosh, and Minas have found that subjects who preferred high probabilities of winning a small payoff to lower probabilities of winning a higher payoff "displayed greater fear of failure . . . than high payoff subjects" (64, p. 27) and also were higher in need achievement. Those who felt a need to achieve success chose those alternatives having the least risk. Phelan (59) used undergraduates playing a business game and found those who possessed a high "cautiousness" personality factor, as measured by a personality test, would take less risk in their decisions and more time to make them. In other words, some people are just more cautious than others and their cautiousness overrides any notions of maximizing subjectively expected utility. Some people enjoy taking risks, others do not.

Of course, the mathematical decision models are much more complicated than indicated not only in their formulation but also in measuring the various parameters of the model. While these models are limited, they are still capable of predicting some aspects of human decision making. It is possible several different models can predict the same decision-making behavior; the real question is whether they describe the *true* behavior individuals are conscious of using.

DECISION MAKING REFERENCES

1. Alberoni, Francesco. Contribution to the study of subjective probability. I. *The Journal of General Psychology* 1962, 66, 241–264.

2. Anderson, Scarvia B. Problem solving in multiple-goal situations. *Journal of Experimental Psychology* 1957, 54, 297–303.

3. Argyris, Chris. *Interpersonal Competence and Organizational Effectiveness.* Homewood, Illinois: Richard D. Irwin, Inc., 1962.

4. Bakke, E. Wight. Concept of the social organization. In *Modern Organization Theory* by Mason Haire (ed.). New York: John Wiley & Sons, Inc., 1959.

5. Bales, Robert F. and Strodtbeck, Fred L. Phases in group problem solving. In *Group Dynamics* by Dorwin Cartwright and Alvin Zander. Evanston, Ill.: Row, Peterson & Company, 1960. (Also in *Journal of Abnormal and Social Psychology,* 1951, 46, 485–495.)

6. Barnlund, Dean C. A comparative study of individual majority, and group judgment. *Journal of Abnormal and Social Psychology* 1959, 58, 55–60.

7. Bavelas, Alex. Communication patterns in task-oriented groups. *Journal of the Acoustical Society of America* 1950, 22, 725–730.

8. Brim, O. G. Jr.; Glass, D. S.; Lavin, D. E. and Goodman, N. *Personality and Decision Processes.* Stanford, California: Stanford University Press, 1962.

9. Cohen, John; Dearnaley, E. J. and Hansel, C. E. M. The addition of subjective probabilities. *Acta Psychologica* 1956, 12, 371–380.

10. Coombs, C. H. and Komorita, S. S. Measuring utility of money through decisions. *American Journal of Psychology* 1958, 71, 383–389.

11. —— and Pruitt, D. G. Components of risk in decision making: probability and variance preferences. *Journal of Experimental Psychology* 1960, 60, 265–277.

12. Cowen, Emory L. The influence of varying degrees of psychological stress on problem-solving rigidity. *Journal of Abnormal and Social Psychology* 1952, 47, 512–519.

13. Cyert, Richard M. and March, James G. *A Behavioral Theory of the Firm.* Englewood Cliffs, New Jersey: Prentice-Hall, Inc., 1963.

14. Danielson, Lee E. and Maier, Norman R. F. Supervisory problems in decision making. *Personnel Psychology* 1957, 10, 169–180.

15. Dean, Burton V. Operations research and managerial decision making. *Administrative Science Quarterly* 1958, 3, 412–428.

16. Deutsch, Karl W. and Madow, William G. A note on the appearance of wisdom in large bureaucratic organizations. *Behavioral Science* 1961, 6, 72–78.

17. Duncan, Carl P. Recent research on human problem solving. *Psychological Bulletin* 1959, 56, 397–429.

18. Dunnette, Marvin D.; Campbell, John and Jaastad, Kay. The effect of group participation on brain-storming effectiveness for two industrial samples. *Journal of Applied Psychology* 1963, 47, 30–37.

19. Edwards, Ward. Probability preferences in gambling. *American Journal of Psychology* 1953, 66, 349–364.

20. ——. Probability preferences among bets with differing expected values. *American Journal of Psychology* 1954, 67, 56–67.

21. ——. The reliability of probability preferences. *American Journal of Psychology* 1954, 67, 68–95.

22. ——. The theory of decision making. *Psychological Bulletin* 1954, 51, 380–417.

23. ——. The prediction of decisions among bets. *Journal of Experimental Psychology* 1955, 50, 201–214.

24. ——. Measurement of utility and subjective probability. In *Psychological Scaling* by H. Gulliksen and S. Messick (ed.). New York: John Wiley & Sons, Inc., 1960.

25. ——. Behavioral decision theory. *Annual Review of Psychology* 1961, 12, 473–498.

26. Ehrlich, Danuta; Guttman, Isaiah; Schonback, Peter and Mills, Judson. Post-decision exposure to relevant information. *Journal of Abnormal and Social Psychology* 1957, 54, 98–102.

27. Ellsberg, Daniel. Risk, ambiguity and the Savage axioms. *Quarterly Journal of Economics* 1961, 75, 643–669.

28. Faust, William L. Group versus individual problem-solving. *Journal of Abnormal and Social Psychology* 1959, 59, 68–72.

29. Festinger, Leon and Aronson, Elliot. The arousal and reduction of dissonance in social contexts. In *Group Dynamics* by Dorwin Cartwright and Alvin Zander (ed.). Evanston, Illinois: Row, Peterson & Company, 1960.

30. Forehand, Garlie A. and Guetzkow, Harold. Judgment and decision-making activities of government executives as described by superiors and co-workers. *Management Science* 1962, 8, 359–370.

31. Gagne, Robert M. Problem solving and thinking. *Annual Review of Psychology* 1959, 10, 147–172.

32. Gore, William J. and Silander, Fred S. A bibliographical essay on decision making. *Administrative Science Quarterly* 1959, 4, 97–121.

33. Guetzkow, Harold and Gyr, John. An analysis of conflict in decision-making groups. *Human Relations* 1954, 7, 367–382.

34. Gurnee, Herbert. A comparison of collective and individual judgments of fact. *Journal of Experimental Psychology* 1937, 21, 106–112.

35. Hall, Ernest J.; Mouton, Jane S. and Blake, Robert R. Group problem solving effectiveness under conditions of pooling vs. interaction. *Journal of Social Psychology* 1963, 59, 147–157.

36. Hare, A. Paul. *Handbook of Small Group Research*. New York: Free Press of Glencoe, Inc., 1962.

37. Hoffman, L. Richard. Conditions for creative problem solving. *The Journal of Psychology* 1961, 52, 429–444.

38. —— and Smith, Clagett G. Some factors affecting the behaviors of members of problem-solving groups. *Sociometry* 1960, 23, 273–291.

39. —— and Maier, Norman R. F. The use of group decision to resolve a problem of fairness. *Personnel Psychology* 1959, 12, 545–559.

40. ————. Quality and acceptance of problem solutions by members of homogeneous and heterogeneous group. *Journal of Abnormal and Social Psychology* 1961, 62, 401–407.

41. Husband, R. W. Cooperative versus solitary problem solution. *Journal of Social Psychology* 1940, 11, 405–409.

42. Kelley, Harold H. and Thibaut, John W. Experimental studies of group problem solving and process. In *Handbook of Social Psychology* by Gardner Lindzey (ed.). Cambridge, Mass.: Addison-Wesley Publishing Co., Inc., 1954.

43. Litchfield, Edward H. Notes on a general theory of administration. *Administrative Science Quarterly* 1956, 1, 3–29.

44. Littig, Lawrence W. Effects of skill and chance orientations on probability preferences. *Psychological Reports* 1962, 10, 67–70.

45. Lorge, Irving; Aikman, L.; Moss, Gilda; Spiegel, J. and Tuckman, J. Solutions by teams and by individuals to a field problem at different levels of reality. *Journal of Educational Psychology* 1955, 46, 17–24.

46. ———; Fox, D.; Davitz, J. and Brenner, M. A survey of studies contrasting the quality of group performance and individual performance. *Psychological Bulletin* 1958, 55, 337–372.

47. ——— and Solomon, Herbert. Individual performance and group performance in problem solving related to group size and previous exposure to the problem. *The Journal of Psychology* 1959, 48, 107–114.

48. Luce, R. Duncan. *Individual Choice Behavior.* New York: John Wiley & Sons, Inc., 1959.

49. ——— and Raiffa, Howard. *Games and Decisions.* New York: John Wiley & Sons, Inc., 1957.

50. McCurdy, H. G. and Lambert, W. E. The efficiency of small human groups in the solution of problems requiring genuine co-operation. *Journal of Personality* 1952, 20, 478–494.

51. Maier, Norman R. F. and Solem, Allen R. Improving solutions by turning choice situations into problems. *Personnel Psychology* 1962, 15, 151–157.

52. Mann, Floyd C. and Williams, Laurence K. Observations on the dynamics of a change to electronic data-processing equipment. *Administrative Science Quarterly* 1960, 5, 217–256.

53. March, James G. and Simon, Herbert A. *Organizations.* New York: John Wiley & Sons, Inc., 1958.

54. Marquart, Dorothy I. Group problem solving. *Journal of Social Psychology* 1955, 41, 103–113.

55. Marschak, Jacob. Elements for a theory of teams. *Management Science* 1955, 1, 127–137.

56. Merrifield, P. R.; Guilford, J. P.; Christensen, P. R. and Frick, J. W. The role of intellectual factors in problem solving. *Psychological Monographs* 1962, 76(10), Whole No. 529.

57. Mills, Judson; Aronson, Elliot and Robinson, Hal. Selectivity in exposure to information. *Journal of Abnormal and Social Psychology* 1959, 59, 250–253.

58. Mosteller, Frederick and Nogee, Philip. An experimental measurement of utility. *Journal of Political Economy* 1951, 59, 371–404.

59. Phelan, Joseph G. An exploration of some personality correlates to business risk-taking behavior. *The Journal of Psychology* 1962, 53, 281–287.

60. Porter, Donald E. Two experiments on group decision making: are *n* heads better than one? *Journal of Industrial Engineering* 1963, 14, 67–72.

61. Radner, Roy. The application of linear programming to team decision problems. *Management Science* 1959, 5, 143–150.

62. Riecken, Henry W. The effect of talkativeness on ability to influence group solutions of problems. *Sociometry* 1958, 21, 309–321.

63. Roby, Thornton. Utility and futurity. *Behavioral Science,* 1962, 7, 194–210.

64. Scodel, Alvin; Ratoosh, Philburn and Minas, J. Sayer. Some personality correlates of decision making under condtions of risk. *Behavioral Science* 1959, 4, 19–28.

65. Shaw, Marvin E. Some effects of problem complexity upon problem solution efficiency in different communication nets. *Journal of Experimental Psychology* 1954, 48, 211–217.

66. ——. Some effects of varying amounts of information exclusively possessed by a group member upon his behavior in the group. *The Journal of General Psychology* 1963, 68, 71–79.

67. —— and Penrod, William T., Jr. Does more information available to a group always improve group performance? *Sociometry* 1962, 25, 377–390.

68. ——; Rothschild, Gerard H. and Strickland. John F. Decision processes in communication nets. *Journal of Abnormal and Social Psychology* 1957, 54, 323–330.

69. Shaw, Marjorie. A comparison of individuals and small groups in the rational solution of complex problems. *American Journal of Psychology* 1932, 44, 491–504.

69a. Shubik, Martin (ed.). *Game Theory and Related Approaches to Social Behavior.* New York: John Wiley & Sons, Inc., 1964.

70. Simon, Herbert A. *Administrative Behavior.* New York: The Macmillan Company, 1957.

71. Slater, Philip E. Contrasting correlates of group size. *Sociometry* 1958, 21, 129–139.

72. Tannenbaum, Robert. Managerial decision-making. *The Journal of Business* 1950, 23, 22–39.

73. Taylor, Donald W. and Faust, William L. Twenty questions: efficiency in problem solving as a function of size of group. *Journal of Experimental Psychology* 1952, 44, 360–368.

74. —— and McNemar, Olga W. Problem solving and thinking. *Annual Review of Psychology* 1955, 6, 455–482.

75. ——; Berry, Paul C. and Block, Clifford H. Does group participation when using brainstorming facilitate or inhibit creative thinking? *Administrative Science Quarterly* 1958, 3, 23–47.

76. Teichner, Warren H. Psychological concepts of probability. *Psychological Reports* 1962, 10, 3–9.

77. Torrance, E. Paul. Methods of conducting critiques of group problem-solving performance. *Journal of Applied Psychology* 1953, 37, 394–398.

78. ——. Group decision-making and disagreement. *Social Forces* 1956, 35, 314–318.

79. ——. Some consequences of power differences on decision making in permanent and temporary three-man groups. In *Small Groups* by A. Paul Hare, Edgar F. Borgatta and Robert F. Bales (eds.). New York: Alfred A. Knopf, Inc., 1955.

80. Van Buskirk, Charles. Performance on complex reasoning tasks as a function of anxiety. *Journal of Abnormal and Social Psychology* 1961, 62, 201–209.

81. Von Neumann, John and Morgenstern, Oskar. *Theory of Games and Economic Behavior*. Princeton, N.J.: Princeton University Press, 1953.

82. Vroom, Victor H. Some personality determinants of the effects of participation. *Journal of Abnormal and Social Psychology* 1959, 59, 322–327.

83. Wallach, Michael A.; Kogan, Nathan and Bem, Daryl J. Group influence on individual risk taking. *Journal of Abnormal and Social Psychology* 1962, 65, 75–86.

84. Wapner, S. and Alper, Thelma G. The effect of an audience on behavior in a choice situation. *Journal of Abnormal and Social Psychology* 1952, 47, 222–229.

85. Wasserman, Paul and Silander, Fred S. *Decision-Making. An Annotated Bibliography*. Ithaca, New York: Cayuga Press, 1958.

86. Willner, Dorothy (ed.) *Decisions, Values and Groups*. New York: Pergamon Press, 1960.

87. Ziller, Robert C. Four techniques of group decision making under uncertainty. *Journal of Applied Psychology* 1957, 41, 384–388.

88. ———. Group size: a determinant of the quality and stability of group decisions. *Sociometry* 1957, 20, 165–173.

89. ——— and Behringer, Richard D. Assimilation of the knowledgeable newcomer under conditions of group success and failure. *Journal of Abnormal and Social Psychology* 1960, 60, 288–291.

5 Communications

Introduction

Communication is, of course, a sharing of information between at least two people. All organizational behavior depends upon communication because attitudes and behavior are themselves forms of communication. Communication is seldom random—a definite audience is usually in mind. Just as no organization can reach its goals without some decision making, so no decision can be made without communication (information) about alternative pathways. Furthermore, the decision to be implemented must be communicated. "A decision occurs upon the receipt of some kind of communication, it consists of a complicated process of combining communications from various sources, and it results in the transmission of further communication" (17, p. 309).

There are many problems that the organization is faced with, but they can all be summed up under three major headings according to Weiss (57): allocation, adaptation, and coordination. Allocation involves determining the "responsibility for particular functional activities" (p. 64); adaptation means developing an "acceptance of responsibility by the member of the organization" (p. 64); coordination involves bringing into harmony "the functional activities of the members" (p. 64). It is this latter problem that particularly relates to communications, though all of the other problems cannot be overcome without the proper hierarchical communication. The concern here is not specifically with how to communicate more effectively [see Sexton (47)] but rather with what variables relate to communication at all levels.

The output of computers has added greatly to the amount of information present in organizations. To do anyone any good, this information has to be communicated and acted upon. The increase in information generated, plus the natural growth in personnel, makes the problem of coordination of parts difficult. Bavelas has said, "the elaboration of communication and control systems . . . has been motivated by the need to find ways in which the human limitations on dealing with great volumes of information speedily and accurately can be overcome" (5, p. 130). Communication is both an individual and an organizational problem. Individuals with certain personality problems, such as a lack of social skills, may be to blame for communication inefficiencies; however, the organizational structure, the way in which information is communicated, may put even more severe limits on communication efficiency. That is, some of the "standard operating procedures" may operate to hinder the organization's pursuit of goals. In fact, Worthy (59) reports that research done by Sears, Roebuck and Company on over 100,000 employees indicates quite clearly that "overcomplexity of organizational structure is one of the most important and fundamental causes of poor management–employee relationships" (p. 174). Too many controls, or restrictions on all forms of communication, can hinder self-reliance and initiative, says Worthy. In any case, it can lead at best to misunderstanding between hierarchies or at worst to no understanding at all.

The impact the communication structure can have upon the individuals in it is brought out clearly by Argyris (2, 3). Based on a company employing about 300 people, he finds that employees in high-skilled jobs as compared to those in low-skilled jobs: "1. Aspire for high quality work. . . . 2. Express high interest in their actual jobs. 3. Express low emphasis on money (as long as present wages are viewed as being fair). 4. Express a sense of self-worth. . . . 5. Show low spoilage of work. 6. Develop strong and lasting friendships. 7. Participate in creative activities outside the plant" (3, pp. 166–167). This is to say that the organization has communicated to its employees that it respects them as individuals by giving them high-skilled jobs. In turn, these employees have communicated to management their appreciation of this fact by points 1, 2, 3, and 5 above. The assumption is, of course, that these points are the result of high-skilled jobs and not the cause of being given them. Argyris says that many organizations do not allow, that is, the structure does not permit, individuals to have sufficient breadth or growth in their work. Hence, employees set up informal structures (not sanctioned by the organization), decrease their efficiency, and become apathetic toward their work; management then strengthens its controls and the problem becomes worse (2, pp. 20–23).

In terms of personality theory, Argyris (2) shows that in our society the development of a human being from child to adult is indicated by similar changes from: (1) "being passive . . . to a state of increasing activity"; (2) developing "from a state of dependence upon others . . . to a state of relative independence"; (3) "being capable of behaving in only a few ways . . . to being capable of behaving in many different ways"; (4) "having erratic, casual, shallow . . . interests . . . to possessing a deepening of interests"; (5) "having a short-time perspective . . . to having a much longer time perspective . . . (the individual's behavior is more affected by the past and the future)"; (6) "being in a subordinate position . . . to aspiring to occupy at least an equal and/or super-ordinate position relative to his peers"; (7) "having a lack of awareness of the self . . . to having an awareness of and control over the self" (pp. 3–4). Organizational structures that do not allow this development frustrate employees thereby producing the effects (apathy, etc.) mentioned previously. On a more specific level, the size of a group can affect the communication structure of its members. Mills (41) has shown that a group of three often breaks up into a pair and a third person; the third person becomes an isolate and often serves as the scapegoat. Here, the isolate is frustrated—the same results as Argyris obtains but due to a different cause. In short, many different situations can produce the same results.

Hierarchical Communication Patterns

It is often said that information flows up the hierarchy and orders flow down, implying one-way communication between management and the worker. This vertical communication is often inversely proportional to horizontal communication within a particular hierarchical level. Simpson (54) presents evidence from a textile mill to show that about 40% of the contacts among a hierarchy of foremen were horizontal. He says that "a critical variable in the direction of communication is apparently the degree of mechanization of the work process" (p. 188). For instance, he says mechanization in the form of the traditional assembly line "reduces the need for close supervision (vertical communication), since instead of the foreman the machines set the work pace" (p. 196); presumably horizontal communications would increase. Conversely, low mechanization would produce high vertical communications because supervision would be closer at all levels; thus, foremen would communicate more with their superiors.

Blau and Scott (9, p. 135) find that data from their analysis of a welfare agency indicated that work pressures increased the frequency with which colleagues consulted each other (horizontal communication) about their professional problems. They point up the fact that usually asking a peer for help creates differences in informal status. "By recurrently requesting a colleague's advice, a person socially acknowledges that the other's standing as an expert is superior to his own . . . receiving advice creates social obligations" (p. 134)*. In the actual study, however, these reciprocal consultation relationships did not result in social obligations because of the pre-established structure.

Communication with a superior can often be done merely to increase one's chances of success, for example, by getting "to be known" by one's superior. Mellinger reports a person "may try to put himself in a more favorable light with [a superior] by minimizing actual disagreement" (40, p. 304) in communication between them. In a study done in three large industrial organizations, Read found that information communicated up the hierarchy is screened or filtered, particularly "when the information content is of a type which might reflect negatively upon the competence and thus, indirectly, upon the security or progress of members of the subordinate level" (45, p. 3). He found a negative correlation between the upward mobility aspirations of persons and "the accuracy with which these members communicate upward in the hierarchy" (p. 4). A low trust of superiors also results in filtering information that is destined to go up, but high trust (i.e., when there are high mobility aspirations) does not reduce this filtering (p. 13). Mellinger finds similar results if communication is with a distrusted person, for then the "primary goal of communication . . . becomes the reduction of one's own anxiety, rather than the accurate transmission of ideas" (40, p. 304). Cohen puts it another way by saying that where low-ranking members of an organization are in a position to move upward in the hierarchy and "if persons of high rank mediate this movement by passing judgments on their performance, we may expect those of low rank to be exceedingly careful in their relations with those of high rank" (16, p. 42). These results are based on a laboratory group of college students but agree with the other studies.

Cohen (16) also found that those persons considered mobile, i.e. able to move up the hierarchy, were communicating more task-relevant information to the upper levels of higher ranking personnel than to nonmobile persons, who communicated with each other. Carrying this type of experi-

* From *Formal Organizations: A Comparative Study* by Peter M. Blau and W. Richard Scott, published by the Chandler Publishing Company, San Francisco. Copyright © 1962 by Chandler Publishing Company. Reprinted by permission.

ment one step further, Kelley found for another laboratory group "communications in the form of substitutes for actual locomotion tend to be initiated by persons who are in low and undesirable positions and who have strong desires to locomote upward" (30, p. 48) but cannot. Presumably what the nonmobiles communicate upward, to be consistent with Cohen's finding, is task irrelevant information. As would be expected, the nonmobile groups are often hostile toward their superiors. And those who are mobile are hostile to each other to some extent, since they represent a threat to each other. Using as subjects people working in the mental hygiene area (social workers, nurses, psychologists, psychiatrists), Hurwitz, Zander, and Hymovitch report that people in the low status positions behave in such a way "to reduce the feelings of uneasiness experienced in their relations with highs . . . to like highs, to overrate the extent to which highs like them, to communicate infrequently and, when they do talk, to talk mainly to highs" (28, p. 808). Because of their low status, little communication will flow down the line.

Changes in Behavior of Groups

Maier has said "the experimental evidence on group decision thus far indicates that a solution worked out by a group is more acceptable to the group than one imposed on the group by an authority" (39, p. 156). In other words, changes in group behavior are accomplished not by a lecture method (imposition by an authority) but by group discussion methods. One of the early experiments in this area was done by Lewin (37). For six groups (ranging in size from 13 to 17) of women volunteers in a home nursing course, half of the groups were exposed to lectures and the other half had discussion groups, the subject of which was the adoption of unpopular meats (sweetbreads, etc.) in home cooking. He checked later with both sets of groups and found 3% of the lecture groups and 32% of the discussion groups used the unpopular meats. However, since only the discussion groups were told their behavior would be checked on later, the results may be biased in favor of the discussion groups. Two other similar experiments were tried with the same results. Lewin explains his findings by pointing out that lectures are passive activities while a discussion "is likely to lead to a much higher degree of involvement" (p. 202) and, hence, a change in behavior. Levine and Butler (36) used lecture and discussion methods with 29 manufacturing supervisors who had made inaccurate merit ratings (job evaluations) of their subordinates in an attempt to improve their ratings. "Only the group of supervisors involved in group decision improved in their ratings" (p. 32).

In a factory situation, some of the worker groups discussed their production goals and others actually set their goals (34). The groups which actually set their production goals showed a greater increase in productivity than the discussion groups. A now classic study by Coch and French (12) in a pajama factory in the South first found this effect in studying resistance to change. Their results indicated that total participation in decision making causes the greatest change in behavior. For clerical workers in an industrial organization, Morse and Reimer found an "increased role in decision making for rank-and-file groups increases their productivity" (42, p. 120). The decision-making role performs the same function as a discussion—it allows personal involvement in the decision to change behavior.

Using college undergraduates in a lecture versus discussion experiment, Bennett (6) reports "group discussion, as an influence technique, was *not* found to be more effective inducement to action than a lecture" (p. 271). This is contrary to the previous studies and can, perhaps, as the author suggests, be explained by group cohesiveness forces. It is possible that the group discussion group had a high degree of cohesiveness with a norm against changing behavior before the experiment actually started. Another interesting finding of hers is "a decision [to change one's behavior] indicated by a public commitment was *not* found to be more effective in assuring the execution of the decision than one indicated less publicly" (p. 271).

Attitude Change

This section is concerned with changes in attitude as opposed to changes in behavior; the two are related but not identical. A claim that a change in attitude will lead to a change in behavior remains to be demonstrated. Just as the way in which a communication asking for a change in behavior affected its outcome, so also will it affect attitude change. The subject of attitude change is so enormous that only that part which relates to organizational behavior will be covered here.

Using groups of 5 college students per group, Pennington, Haravey, and Bass (43) had them perform a decision-making task under differing experimental conditions: group discussion, group decision and/or no discussion at all. They found increased agreement on the solution to the task when there was discussion; the "change of opinion was significantly greater for groups permitted either discussion or decision . . . greatest change occurred when both were permitted" (p. 407). As with changing behavior, group discussion is effective in changing attitudes. It could be argued that a larger group would be more effective in changing attitudes since more opinions and points of view would be presented than in a smaller group. However, it is also possible to argue that too many opinions could confuse the issue. Rath and Misra (44) designed an experiment with undergraduates to resolve the dilemma. The subjects were put into discussion groups of 3, 7, and 11 members each to observe changes in attitudes. "Though there was considerable change of attitudes in each group size . . . this effect is maximally seen in group size 7. Group size 3 and group size 11 do not differ significantly from each other" (p. 256). Apparently three people do not produce enough opinion to influence, relative to seven, and eleven produce too much.

Influencing individual attitudes can often be done in subtle ways. For instance, an overheard communication can effectively influence opinions, since "defenses against new ideas are presumably weaker because preconceptions are not so pervasively present" (7, p. 458). As Berelson has said, there are certain "psychological advantages centering around the gratification of 'overhearing something not meant for you'" (7, p. 458); and as Walster and Festinger put it, overheard conversation is effective in attitude change because "the speaker cannot possibly be seen as intending to influence the listener" (56, p. 395). They set up an experiment whereby some of the subjects overheard a conversation concerning smoking and cancer, while the other subjects listened specifically to the same conversation, i.e., they knew those talking knew they were present. Part of the subjects were smokers, part were not. Those who overheard the conversation, i.e. those who felt the talkers did not know of their presence, changed their attitudes about smoking and cancer more than did the other group, with the smokers in each case influenced the most. "When the issue was an involving one for the group, the overheard communication would be especially effective. When the issue was not involving, the difference between the overheard and regular conditions was expected to be small" (p. 402). Perhaps, what the person overhears in an organization is responsible for more attitude changes than formal attempts.

Forewarning about a potentially persuasive piece of communication can often affect the results of the communication. Kiesler and Kiesler (31) had 187 male and female undergraduates read a paper strongly advocating more foreign aid. One-third of the subjects had a note at the end of the paper saying it was designed to change opinion (afterwarned condition); one-third had the same note at the beginning of the paper (forewarned); and the remaining subjects had no warning about the paper's intent. The results indicated, "if the subject is not informed of the propagandistic intent of the communication until after he has read it, then the warning has no effect" (p. 549). This happens, probably, because the communication is internalized before the warning is. Forewarning, though, "had the effect of nullifying the persuasive communication" (p. 549), because forewarning came before the content could be internalized. It appears we believe a part of everything we read unless warned previously. Allyn and Festinger used high school students in a situation concerning the exertion of more control over teenagers and found "subjects who were forewarned of the nature of the communication changed their opinions less and rejected the communicator as biased" (1, p. 40). In an experiment by Fine (18), college students read an article on biological warfare. Half of the articles ended with a specific conclusion while the other half did not; except for the ending all articles said the same thing. He found the article with a definite conclusion to be more effective in changing attitudes (p. 374). As might be expected, those with little initial concern about the topic were influenced more than those who had initial opinions about it. He also found that high anxiety subjects, regardless of initial opinions, changed their opinion more than those low in anxiety (p. 374), perhaps, because they were less stable emotionally and were more easily swayed.

Cognitive dissonance arises, say Allyn and Festinger (1), when a person is exposed to a communication that differs in opinion from his own. To reduce the dissonance between his and the other's opinion "he can change his opinion to a position closer to that advocated . . . or he can reject and derogate the communication and the communicator" (p. 35). This explains quite well most of the effects encountered in the area of attitude change. One situation where it is not particularly applicable is a fear-arousing one. Janis and Feshback (29) gave three different lectures on dental hygiene to three different groups of high school students. One of the lectures (strong appeal) was fear-arousing and stated that "pain, disease, body damage" would result if the teeth were not cared for. The moderate appeal was more mild and the minimal appeal "rarely referred to the unpleasant consequences." All appeals contained the same basic information and recommendations. The fear-arousing appeal caused the most worry, but the "greatest amount of conformity to the communicator's recommendations was produced by the minimal appeal" (p. 92). A strong fear appeal is not very effective in maintaining attitude change over an extended time period.

An interesting question to ask about two conflicting communications is, "Does it make any difference which one is presented first in influencing an opinion?" A primacy effect is one where the communication presented first changes opinion, and a recency effect is one where the argument presented last has the greater effect. Lana states that the early studies "indicated that neither a primacy nor a recency effect is immediately evident in the situation where two communications on a single topic, one affirmative and the other negative, are presented successively" (32, p. 573). There is some evidence now that under certain conditions, primacy has the greatest effect. Hovland (27) lists the conditions when primacy is more influential: "when cues as to the incompatibility of different items of information are absent . . . when the contradictory information is presented by the same communicator . . . when the issue is an unfamiliar one . . . when the recipient has only a superficial interest in the issue" (p. 148). Just how unfamiliar the communication has to be for primacy to operate is not clear yet. Lana finds "a recency effect . . . when the subject's familiarity with the topic of communication is near zero" (32, p. 577). With some familiarity with a topic, he finds the communication presented first is more effective in producing attitude change. Combining Hovland's and Lana's findings, we can say that recency operates with virtually no knowledge of the subject, primacy operates with some knowledge, but neither operates with total familiarity. Organizations are interested in changing attitudes and behavior to conform with their goals and norms; this interest affects not only the people within the organization, but, indirectly, all who come in contact with it. Thus, many persons have a stake in the kind of changes made.

Communication Nets

Communication nets or networks refer to the arrangement of communication channels in an organization. An organizational chart depicting the hierarchy of supervision is also a formal communication network showing how information "should" be communicated among the hierarchical levels. Often, of course, the established "chain of command" is not followed. The organizational structure is identical to the communication network. Many researchers have studied organizational structures, for example, Whyte (58) in his study of a restaurant, to determine the official and unofficial allocation of authority and the communication setup. But up to this time (1950) there was no rigorous way of experimenting in the laboratory with communication structures. Then, in 1950 Bavelas (4) presented an experimental procedure for studying communication nets that led to a proliferation of further work. He posed the question if it were possible that "among several communication patterns, all logically adequate for the successful completion of a specified task, one gives significantly better performance?" (p. 726).

Bavelas proposed the communication networks shown in Figure 1. Each letter represents a person and the lines connecting the persons are the communication channels. Communication among the five persons in each net can only take place by the channels indicated. The distances, metrically speaking, between each person can be handled by an index of relative centrality. The index is simply obtained by dividing "the sum of all internal distances of the pattern" by "the total sum of distances for any one position in the pattern." Thus, for the "Y" net in Figure 1 the index would be computed as follows (it is assumed the distance between two adjacent people on the communication channel is a unitless 1):

Distance from p to q = 1	q to p = 1	r to p = 2
p to r = 2	q to r = 1	r to q = 1
p to s = 3	q to s = 2	r to s = 1
p to t = 3	q to t = 2	r to t = 1

"Sum of distances   9   6   5
for any one position
in the pattern"

s to p = 3	t to p = 3	"Sum of all internal
s to q = 2	t to q = 2	distances of the
s to r = 1	t to r = 1	pattern" =
s to t = 2	t to s = 2	$9 + 6 + 5 + 8 + 8 = 36$
8	8	

The centrality index for person p is 36/9, for q it is 36/6, etc. It should be apparent that the larger this number is, the more central is the person in the net.

In this paper, Bavelas presented the actual experimental results, using these nets, of S. L. Smith and H. J. Leavitt. Leavitt's results have also been published elsewhere (35). Smith only used the Circle and Chain structure while Leavitt used all four. Smith had groups of 5 college students sit around a table with each student occupying a cubicle such that each one could only communicate by written messages with those adjacent to him in the net. Their task was to determine what, among six possibilities, was the common symbol on a card among them. He found the person in the most central position is usually seen as the "leader" of the group. He also found the Chain net was more efficient by having the fewer number of errors in solving the problem. Leavitt also found the Chain to have less errors than the Circle. Furthermore, the "Y" net had fewer errors than the Chain but the Wheel had the same number of average errors per group as the "Y." It appeared, then, that the network with the least centralized structure (Circle) had the most errors and the errors decreased as the structure became more centralized, ("Y" and Wheel). As the centralization increased, so too did the agreement on who was the leader (the most central person) and the satisfaction with the group. Those persons most satisfied were the ones who had the highest centrality index in their particular network. "Positions which limit independence of action (peripheral positions) would be unsatisfying" (35, p. 48).

The whole area of communication networks has been reviewed by Glanzer and Glaser (21) and their general approach will be followed. The studies reported by Bavelas were followed the next year by Heise and Miller (26). They used three-man groups in Chain and Circle nets, and unlike

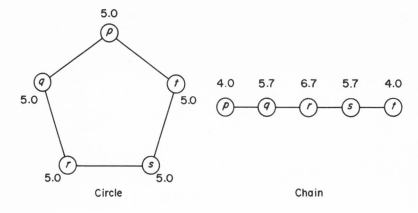

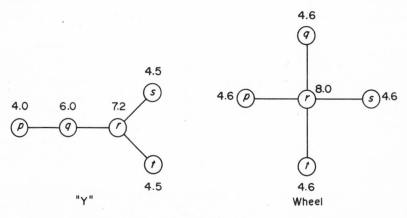

Figure 1. Communication networks reported by Bavelas (4). The relative centrality index of each position for each network is indicated by the number adjacent to each letter.

the Bavelas studies, not all communication was two-way, meaning that in some of the nets, person A could communicate with person B but B could not communicate with A. Communication among members was via an intercom system, and as part of the experiment noise was introduced at times over the system. As the noise level changed and as the task changed so also did the efficiency of the various nets. Glanzer and Glaser have said, "the main contribution of the study is probably that it demonstrates that no network is best in all situations" (21, p. 6).

Leavitt (35) found that the Wheel, "Y," Chain, and Circle in that order had the greatest speed of organizing in performing the tasks. Guetzkow and Simon (24) verified these results by using five-man Wheel, Circle, and All

Channel (the Circle arrangement except every member was connected by a communication channel with *every* other member) nets. They, too, found the Wheel groups needed the least time to organize for effective problem solution since the most central member automatically became the leader. Those in the Circle nets had the most difficulty in organizing since they had to choose a leader and establish relays to him. Intermediate in difficulty was the All Channel net which had to decide on a leader but did not have trouble in establishing relays, since full communication among members obviated the need of relays. Guetzkow and Dill (23) thought that a Circle group if given time to organize via an All Channel net would perform as an All Channel group, but their hypothesis was not supported as the All Channel net continued to perform better.

Using five-man groups in the Wheel, "Y," and Chain nets, Goldberg (22) presented a card with a large number of dots on it and the nets as a whole using the designated channels, had to come to a group decision as to the number of dots. He found that those people in the more central positions were influenced less in their judgment than those in the peripheral ones. Also, those in the more central positions were more often chosen as leaders.

Shaw has continued on with these studies using mostly four-man groups as illustrated in Figure 2. In one study (49) his findings confirm the other studies cited with regard to the relationship of centrality and satisfaction and leadership nominations. In another study, Shaw (51) reports that the Wheel nets needed fewer messages sent than the Slash or Circle nets—all of which is in agreement with Leavitt's early finding. In both Shaw's and Leavitt's experiments, the subjects first had to organize their nets, but where such initial organization is not necessary as in the situation used by Carzo (11), the Circle nets take less time for problem solution than do the Wheels. Even when initial organization is necessary, Shaw (50) finds his four-man Circles a little faster than the Wheel nets, under certain conditions, such as when the problem to solve is complex. With this type of problem the members apparently want to observe all the information, and this is accomplished faster in the Circle. When the problem is simple, the Wheel becomes the fastest as the members do not care to see all the information and send it directly to the central position. For human relations problems, Shaw, Rothschild, and Strickland (53) find the Wheel to be the slowest problem-solving net, the Slash the next slowest, and the All Channel the fastest. If, though, a human relations problem is considered to be complex, then the results would be in agreement with those of Shaw (50).

Shaw (51) used Wheel, Kite, and All Channel nets for arithmetic problem solution. The person in the most central position in each net was designated as the leader by the experimenter. Part of the time the leader was instructed to be autocratic in his behavior and part of the time to be demo-

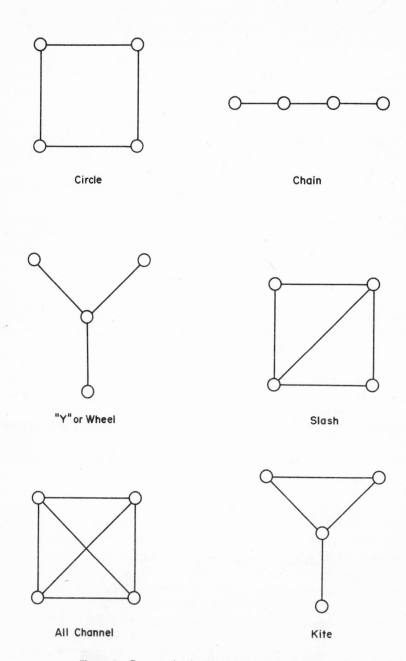

Circle

Chain

"Y" or Wheel

Slash

All Channel

Kite

Figure 2. Communication networks used by Shaw.

cratic. The autocratic leadership produced the better performance but also produced the lowest morale. It could be that a homeostatic or negative feedback phenomenon occurred here. Negative feedback refers to keeping the situation fairly unchanging *in toto* and, in this case, would mean that efficiency increased at the expense of morale but the over-all group product is the same. If this entity called the group product kept constant, then if morale increased, efficiency would decrease. Lyle (38) set up four-man communication nets, where the task was to write an agreed upon news story, under authorization and democratic conditions. He found "democratic groups tended to generate a higher task-relevant communication rate than did authoritarian groups" (p. 373) but also sent more task-irrelevant information back and forth. Berkowitz (8) also used four-man groups in a communication net experiment and varied the position of high ascendance (authoritarian) and low ascendance (democratic) persons in the net. He found that when the low ascendance types were placed in the central-most positions they changed their behavior more than the high ascendance types because of the effect of the task demands. Also, high ascendance persons in the peripheral positions in the net were just as satisfied as the low ascendance types in the periphery. Because of the desire of the high ascendant types to possess authority, one would expect that this type of person would not be as satisfied in this position as a low ascendance type person. But the evidence shows authoritarian types can be placed in the periphery without apparent harm to the group, at least in terms of satisfaction.

Many other communication net studies have been done with somewhat more realistic groups, such as with military groups used by Lanzetta and Roby (33, 46), but the conclusions with regard to satisfaction or morale, leadership, and efficiency are the same. "Morale seems to be a function of centrality of position" (21, p. 18), and there is "leadership status for the central members" (25, p. 277). As for efficiency, whether measured by number of errors or by quality of group decision, "the effect of structure depends in part on the requirements of the task" (21, p. 18). The maximization of efficiency and individual satisfaction has yet to be achieved.

Studying another effect of the types of nets, Ziller (61) found for Air Force bomber crews "the more flexible groups and the more confident groups were generally found to be those with the more open communication systems . . . with relatively fewer restraints on the member's interaction" (p. 351). Cohen and his colleagues (13, 14, 15) have investigated the organizational procedures of groups changed from one network to another. Some of the groups worked first on problem solving in a Wheel net and then were changed to a Circle net. Eighty per cent of the groups reorganized from a Circle to a Chain and solved problems faster than those who had always worked in a Circle net; "of the eight emergent Chains, only one maintained the former leader of the Wheel arrangement" (14, p. 357). Thus, "the election changed the position of the leader from a representative of external authority to a delegate of the authority of the group" (13, p. 456). Other groups worked first in Circle nets, then were changed to Wheels and now they solved problems slower than those who had always worked in a Wheel net. This resulted because the initial Circle experience interfered, a negative transfer of training, with subsequent organization in a theoretically faster net. On the subject of change, Trow (55) investigated the effects of change of personnel in a Circle communication net on problem-solving activity. He had some of the members in the net replaced by new members at different time periods; thus, the number of people replaced and the speed at which they were replaced were the variables. The results "give little or no support to propositions asserting that mean rate of succession in . . . organizations has any regular effect upon long-run team or organizational performance" (p. 266). It is not the number of people replaced, per se, that disrupts performance but rather it is the number replaced per unit time that affects performance, as it disrupts the information-handling procedures (p. 266).

As pointed out, there are many factors that affect performance in communication nets—so many that few definitive statements can be made. Furthermore, the network experiments are conducted under conditions that depart from real-life situations. "Network members know very little about other positions and about behavior of any except adjacent positions . . . this is a condition that does not hold in small groups" (21, p. 19). In most of the network experiments, "each member is essential because each member holds an essential piece of information . . . this is not generally true in real-life groups" (21, p. 19). Glanzer and Glaser argue that "if the network studies have any application, it will not be in the small group, but in a much larger unit such as an industrial corporation or an army" (21, p. 19) because the network conditions resemble more a large organization.

The communication nets discussed are not the only ways to study rigorously the structural properties of groups. For example, a more complex approach is Heider's theory of structural balance elaborated on by Cartwright and Harary (10) and tested in part by Foa (19). This theory is concerned with whether or not individuals have balanced interpersonal relations where balance is defined as, person A likes what his friend B likes, A dislikes what B dislikes and A likes what his "enemy" C dislikes. These relationships are handled by the linear theory of graphs. But this approach, like the communication net studies, has, as yet, contributed little absolute knowledge about behavior under realistic communication situations.

COMMUNICATIONS REFERENCES

1. Allyn, Jane and Festinger, Leon. The effectiveness of unanticipated persuasive communications. *Journal of Abnormal and Social Psychology* 1961, 62, 35–40.

2. Argyris, Chris. The individual and organization: some problems of mutual adjustment. *Administrative Science Quarterly* 1957, 2, 1–24.

3. ———. The individual and organization: an empirical test. *Administrative Science Quarterly* 1959, 4, 145–167.

4. Bavelas, Alex. Communication patterns in task-oriented groups. *Journal of the Acoustical Society of America* 1950, 22, 725–730.

5. ———. Communication and organization. In *Management Organization and the Computer* by George P. Schultz and Thomas L. Whisler (eds.). New York: The Free Press, 1960.

6. Bennett, Edith Becker. Discussion, decision, commitment, and consensus in 'group decision.' *Human Relations* 1955, 8, 251–273.

7. Berelson, B. Communication and public opinion. In *Reader in Public Opinion and Communication* by B. Berelson and M. Janowitz (eds.). New York: The Free Press, 1950.

8. Berkowitz, Leonard. Personality and group position. *Sociometry* 1956, 19, 210–222.

9. Blau, Peter M. and Scott, W. Richard. *Formal Organizations.* San Francisco: Chandler Publishing Co., 1962.

10. Cartwright, Dorwin and Harary, Frank. Structural balance: a generalization of Heider's theory. *Psychological Review* 1956, 63, 277–293.

11. Carzo, Rocco, Jr. Some effects of organization structure on group effectiveness. *Administrative Science Quarterly* 1963, 7, 393–424.

12. Coch, Lester and French, John R. P., Jr. Overcoming resistance to change. *Human Relations* 1948, 1, 512–532.

13. Cohen, Arthur M. Changing small-group communication networks. *Administrative Science Quarterly* 1962, 6, 443–462.

14. ——— and Bennis, Warren G. Continuity of leadership in communication networks. *Human Relations* 1961, 14, 351–367.

15. ——— and Wolkon, George H. The effects of changes in communication networks on the behaviors of problem-solving groups. *Sociometry* 1962, 25, 177–196.

16. Cohen, Arthur R. Upward communication in experimentally created hierarchies. *Human Relations* 1958, 11, 41–53.

17. Dorsey, John T., Jr. A communication model for administration. *Administrative Science Quarterly* 1957, 2, 307–324.

18. Fine, Bernard J. Conclusion—drawing, communicator credibility, and anxiety as factors in opinion change. *Journal of Abnormal and Social Psychology* 1957, 54, 369–374.

19. Foa, Uriel G. Behavior, norms, and social rewards in a dyad. *Behavioral Science* 1958, 3, 323–334.

20. Gilchrist, J. C.; Shaw, Marvin E. and Walker, L. C. Some effects of unequal distribution of information in a wheel group structure. *Journal of Abnormal and Social Psychology* 1954, 49, 554–556.

21. Glanzer, Murray and Glaser, Robert. Techniques for the study of group structure and behavior: II Empirical studies of the effects of structure in small groups. *Psychological Bulletin* 1961, 58, 1–27.

22. Goldberg, S. C. Influence and leadership as a function of group structure. *Journal of Abnormal and Social Psychology* 1955, 51, 119–122.

23. Guetzkow, Harold and Dill, William R. Factors in the organizational development of task-oriented groups. *Sociometry* 1957, 20, 175–204.

24. —— and Simon, Herbert A. The impact of certain communication nets upon organization and performance in task-oriented groups. *Management Science* 1955, 1, 233–250.

25. Hare, A. Paul. *Handbook of Small Group Research.* New York: Free Press of Glencoe, Inc., 1962.

26. Heise, George A. and Miller, George A. Problem solving by small groups using various communication nets. *Journal of Abnormal and Social Psychology* 1951, 46, 327–335.

27. Hovland, Carl I. The role of primacy and recency in persuasive communication. In *Readings in Social Psychology* by Eleanor E. Maccoby, Theodore M. Newcomb and Eugene L. Hartley (eds.). New York: Holt, Rinehart & Winston, Inc., 1958.

28. Hurwitz, Jacob I.; Zander, Alvin F. and Hymovitch, Bernard. Some effects of power on the relations among group members. In *Group Dynamics* by Dorwin Cartwright and Alvin Zander (eds.). Evanston, Ill.: Row, Peterson & Co., 1960.

29. Janis, Irving and Feshback, Seymour. Effects of fear-arousing communications. *Journal of Abnormal and Social Psychology* 1953, 48, 78–92.

30. Kelley, Harold H. Communication in experimentally created hierarchies. *Human Relations* 1951, 4, 39–56.

31. Kiesler, Charles A. and Kiesler, Sara B. Role of forewarning in persuasive communications. *Journal of Abnormal and Social Psychology* 1964, 68, 547–549.

32. Lana, Robert E. Familiarity and the order of presentation of persuasive communications. *Journal of Abnormal and Social Psychology* 1961, 62, 573–577.

33. Lanzetta, John T. and Roby, Thornton B. Group performance as a function of work-distribution patterns and task load. *Sociometry* 1956, 19, 95–104.

34. Lawrence, Lois C. and Smith, Patricia C. Group decision and employee participation. *Journal of Applied Psychology* 1955, 39, 334–337.

35. Leavitt, Harold J. Some effects of certain communication patterns on group performance. *Journal of Abnormal and Social Psychology* 1951, 46, 38–50.

36. Levine, Jacob and Butler, John. Lecture versus group decision in changing behavior. *Journal of Applied Psychology* 1952, 36, 29–33.

37. Lewin, Kurt. Group decision and social change. In *Readings in Social Psychology* by Eleanor E. Maccoby, Theodore M. Newcomb and Eugene L. Hartley (eds.). New York: Holt, Rinehart & Winston, Inc., 1958.

38. Lyle, Jack. Communication, group atmosphere, productivity, and morale in small task groups. *Human Relations* 1961, 14, 369–379.

39. Maier, Norman R. F. The quality of group decisions as influenced by the discussion leader. *Human Relations* 1950, 3, 155–174.

40. Mellinger, Glen D. Interpersonal trust as a factor in communication. *Journal of Abnormal and Social Psychology* 1956, 52, 304–309.

41. Mills, Theodore M. Power relations in three-person groups. *American Sociological Review* 1953, 18, 351–357.

42. Morse, Nancy C. and Reimer, Everett. The experimental change of a major organizational variable. *Journal of Abnormal and Social Psychology* 1956, 52, 120–129.

43. Pennington, D. F., Jr.; Haravey, Francois and Bass, Bernard M. Some effects of decision and discussion on coalescence, change, and effectiveness. *Journal of Applied Psychology* 1958, 42, 404–408.

44. Rath, R. and Misra, S. K. Change of attitudes as a function of size of discussion-groups. *The Journal of Social Psychology* 1963, 59, 247–257.

45. Read, William H. Upward communication in industrial hierarchies. *Human Relations* 1962, 15, 3–15.

46. Roby, Thornton B. and Lanzetta, John T. Conflicting principles in man-machine system design. *Journal of Applied Psychology* 1957, 41, 170–178.

47. Sexton, Richard and Staudt, Virginia. Business communication: a survey of the literature. *The Journal of Social Psychology* 1959, 50, 101–118.

48. Shaw, Marvin E. A comparison of two types of leadership in various communication nets. *Journal of Abnormal and Social Psychology* 1955, 50, 127–134.

49. ———. Group structure and the behavior of individuals in small groups. *Journal of Psychology* 1954, 38, 139–149.

50. ———. Some effects of problem complexity upon problem solution efficiency in different communication nets. *Journal of Experimental Psychology* 1954, 48, 211–217.

51. ———. Some effects of unequal distribution of information upon group performance in various communication nets. *Journal of Abnormal and Social Psychology* 1954, 49, 547–553.

52. ———. Some effects of irrelevant information upon problem-solving by small groups. *The Journal of Social Psychology* 1958, 47, 33–37.

53. ———; Rothschild, Gerard H. and Strickland, John F. Decision processes in communication nets. *Journal of Abnormal and Social Psychology* 1957, 54, 323–330.

54. Simpson, Richard L. Vertical and horizontal communication in formal organizations. *Administrative Science Quarterly* 1959, 4, 188–196.

55. Trow, Donald B. Membership succession and team performance. *Human Relations* 1960, 13, 259–268.

56. Walster, Elaine and Festinger, Leon. The effectiveness of "overheard" persuasive communications. *Journal of Abnormal and Social Psychology* 1962, 65, 395–402.

57. Weiss, Robert S. A structure-function approach to organization. *The Journal of Social Issues* 1956, 12, No. 2, 61–67.

58. Whyte, William Foote. The social structure of the restaurant. *The American Journal of Sociology* 1949, 54, 302–310.

59. Worthy, James C. Organizational structure and employee morale. *American Sociological Review* 1950, 15, 169–179.

60. Zajonc, Robert B. The process of cognitive tuning in communication. *Journal of Abnormal and Social Psychology* 1960, 61, 159–167.

61. Ziller, Robert C. Communication restraints, group flexibility, and group confidence. *Journal of Applied Psychology* 1958, 42, 346–352.

6

Leadership

Introduction

Probably as much has been written about leadership as any other area of organizational behavior. Leadership is present in almost any group, almost by definition, whether it be composed of children, adults, or baboons. The primary concern here will be with adults, although studies involving children will be mentioned if they have been major contributions to the field. Before discussing leadership, we differentiate it from supervision. Supervision is concerned with acts issued from a formal or appointed position in the organization by someone with authority, the "legal" right to act. "Legal," here, means issued officially by the organization. Leadership, on the other hand, concerns acts issued from a formal *or* informal position in the organization by someone with power, the ability to act, which implies nothing about the legal right.

A revolutionary in a country does not have authority, a "legal" right, to take up arms against the government, but he can have the power, or ability, to do so. Of course, both supervision and leadership, as concepts, may occur together and, in fact, it would be desirable for a supervisor to have "leadership"—that is, to have the ability to initiate group goals within the organizational structure. But where the authority is delegated or where it is secondary to ability, the term "supervision" will be in order. A better idea of supervision will be gained by reading Chapter 7, which deals with organizational officials (managers, supervisors, foremen, etc.) acting in their formal capacities.

Power can be thought of as potential influence which accounts for the ability to act in the first place. French and Raven (35) have defined five bases of social power. *Reward* power of O (social agent or potential leader) over P (person) increases as P feels that O can deliver rewards to him. *Coercive* power of O increases as P feels that O can deliver punishments if P fails to respond to the influence attempt. *Referent* power of O over P increases as P identifies more and more with O. *Expert* power exists for O when P sees that O has some expertise on a given subject. *Legitimate* power occurs when P perceives that O has the legal right to determine P's behavior. From what has been said, legitimate power would appear to apply only to supervision—it may even be considered a definition of authority; in terms of leadership, it is not power at all. The four other forms of power, if formalized, would also be forms of authority—if rewards and punishments were set by the organization, if P is attracted to O because of his formal position, if P thinks that O is an expert because of his position. There will be overlap, of course, between supervisory and leadership practices, but usually leadership will refer to those acts over and above those of supervision.

This influence potential of leaders has been discussed by Bennis (16, p. 295) who states, "leadership can be defined as the process by which an agent induces a subordinate to behave in a desired manner" and by Stogdill (71, p. 4) who states, "leadership may be considered as the process (act) of influencing the activities of an organized group in its efforts toward goal setting and goal achievement." Cartwright and Zander (26, p. 496) talk of leadership in the same vein. Cattell (27, p. 176), too, would agree with these main activities of a leader; he states them "(a) helping the group to find the machinery or means to a goal (syntality) already agreed upon and (b) helping the group to decide upon a goal (synergy) that is satisfactory in the sense that the group can stably pursue it." The leader is able to perform these functions because of the group's concurrence, not, like the supervisor, because of their obligation by formal rules to allow him these activities. This is but one approach to defining leadership.

Some of the possible definitions of leadership have been listed by Gibb (36, pp. 880–883): (1) "the leader is an individual in a given office . . . whoever occupies a leader's office is a leader"—this becomes the definition of a supervisor in this chapter's terms; (2) "the leader as focus for the behavior of group members . . . the nature of the emotional relationship between the leader and other group members"; (3) "the leader in terms of sociometric choice . . . preference relationships among the members"—the leader is the one most often chosen by the members in listing preferences of association; (4) "the leader as one who exercises influence over others"; (5) "the leader defined in terms of influence upon syntality"; (6) "the leader as one who engages in leadership behaviors"—a leader is one who possesses certain leadership traits. A seventh definition would involve the leader's concern with group roles. Benne and Sheats (15) have indicated a leader's function is to identify and allocate roles among the group members. Gouldner (40, p. 20) says, "leadership is . . . a role which an individual occupies." Relevant to this notion, Gibb (37, p. 284) has said, "a leader is a member of a group on whom the group confers a certain status, and leadership describes the role by which the duties of this status are fulfilled." The roles each member plays are essentially responsibilities he takes on; Stogdill (72, p. 4) "suggests that leadership cannot emerge unless the members of a group assume different responsibilities." In other terms, "without leadership, there is no focus about which a number of individuals may cluster to form a group" (37, p. 267). As Homans (51, p. 415) has said, "the leader brings his group from one social state to another through giving orders that govern . . . the behavior of the members."

In studying leadership, there has been concern expressed about separating the leadership concept per se from the organizational concept. But if the leader formulates group and, indirectly, organizational goals, he can hardly be studied as an independent phenomenon. "The minimal conditions that permit the existence of leadership are exactly the same variables that define an organization" (73, p. 136); again, "it may not be possible to study leadership phenomenon in an organizational setting without studying the nature of the organization" (1, p. 336). For those studies conducted in a laboratory setting, the group itself is the organization, so no problem of isolation exists. However, in studying real groups (permanent groups existing within an organization) an insoluble problem does arise—studying the whole organization introduces variables that cannot be controlled. The importance of organizational variables is realized, however, and they are studied as they affect the group. The important variables of leadership, according to Gibb (36, p. 914) are: (1) "the personality of the leader"—i.e., his traits; (2) "the followers with their attitudes, needs, and problems"— one is a leader by virtue of those followers who allow this position to exist; (3) "the group itself both as regards (a) structure of interpersonal relations and (b) syntality characteristics"—the organization of the group; (4) "the situations as determined by physical setting"—the environmental effects. The first two relate primarily to leadership traits, and the latter two primarily to the situation. They are evidence of two different approaches—one leader-oriented (from the leader to the situation), the other situation-oriented (from the situation to the leader). Whyte (79) has done a most interesting study of a street gang in the Boston area in the 1930's, which incorporates

[handwritten annotation: Physical characteristics and personality (alertness, cheerfulness, geniality) — little relationship to leadership]

both approaches. Other more general leadership review articles have been done by Bavelas (10), Gibb (36), and Tannenbaum and Massarik (75).

Leadership Traits

Stogdill (72) and Gibb (36) mention in articles reviewing many leadership studies that such traits as height, weight, appearance, self-control, dominance, surgency (alertness, cheerfulness, geniality), and intelligence have little relationship to leadership. For instance, as regards intelligence, "lower than (group) average intelligence inhibits access to leadership, but higher than average intelligence is no guarantee of leadership" (40, p. 33). Studies of leadership progressed from identifying the physical characteristics of leaders to the analysis of their personality traits. Bonner (18, p. 167) has stated that the relationship between physical factors and leadership "probably varies with the type of leadership activity performed." A gang of juvenile delinquents intent upon doing physical damage to others will choose as its leader the one who has the necessary physical attributes; in this case the correlation between leadership and height and weight and strength traits would be high. As soon as the group goal changed, though, these leaderships traits would probably no longer be relevant. "While individual traits cannot be ignored, a knowledge of the individual leader yields a very imperfect understanding of leadership itself" (18, p. 176). One of the early leadership trait studies (29) involved 112 subjects composed of student, criminal (from prisons) and U. S. Army leaders. They were all given several psychological tests, and it was found they had the following traits in common: self-confidence, speed in reaching a decision, and finality of judgment.

The "great man" theory of leadership rests upon the presence of leadership traits and predicts that "changes in social or group life are effected by men of uncommon talents or abilities" (18, p. 165). Borgatta, Bales and Couch (21) define the "great man" as the all-around leader. In their experiment they used 126 Air Force men in groups of three, arranged so that each group contained men of equal rank, to eliminate problems of authority. On the basis of tasks the group engaged in, researchers selected the all-around leaders and put them into different groups at the conclusion of each of four further group tasks. No "great man" ever served with group members with whom he had previously worked nor were two "great" men ever put together. The authors state that the "stability with which great men, chosen on the basis of their first session performance, retain top position in subsequent groups is impressive" (p. 759). Since there were three persons in each group, the probability of any one person being its leader is $\frac{1}{3}$; the probability of this same person being the leader in the second group he is in is $\frac{1}{3} \cdot \frac{1}{3}$ or $\frac{1}{9}$. For the four groups used, the probability of the same man being the leader each time is $(\frac{1}{3})^4$ or $\frac{1}{81}$. This experiment's conclusion would be that a person can be an all-around leader in groups composed of different members doing quite similar tasks, i.e., where the situation remains essentially the same from group to group. This implies leadership traits are relative to the situation to some extent. Bell and French (13) used 25 male undergraduates in groups of five, changing them so each person appeared only once with every other person. Each time a group met it discussed a different human relations case; at the end of the discussion session, it nominated a discussion leader for "a hypothetical second meeting of the same group." The leadership status a person had was the average of the four rankings he was given by the other group members in making a choice of a future discussion leader. The correlation between the leadership status a person had in the first set of groups he was in and that in the remaining groups was significant, indicating "individual characteristics are responsible for somewhat over half . . . of the variance in leadership status within the average group" (p. 766). But as the authors indicate, "this finding cannot be generalized to all types of groups."

Carter, Haythorn, and Howell (24) used 36 college students in groups doing reasoning, clerical (sorting of cards), and discussion-type tasks. Their results indicate "leadership is not completely specific but rather, from knowing that a person was a leader on one of the tasks, we can predict that he will tend to be a leader on other tasks" (p. 353). Katz, et al. (55) have suggested, "that leaders change not with every change of activity, but only with changes to markedly different kinds of activity—that is, to activities which may no longer be compatible with the leader's talents" (p. 37). An example of this would be that, "leaders in Officer Candidate School often fail to retain their leadership in combat." The obvious tactic for leaders, then, is to perpetuate that activity within which their leadership has existed without competition. Whyte, in writing of the street corner gang he studied, says of its leader, "it is natural for him to promote activities in which he excels and to discourage those in which he is not skillful" (79, p. 259). Katz, et al. used three- and four-person groups of teenagers, matched by age and sex, in a total of 39 groups to test the hypothesis: "Leadership will be more likely to remain stable when a group has its own way about 'elaborating the range of its activities' than if new demands are thrust upon the group from outside" (55, p. 40). Their finding was that a task imposed from outside the group did cause a change in leaders. A leader steers his group's attitudes and preferences toward his own so he can maintain leadership—alternatively, the group expects the leader will have their preferences. The outside demands imposed upon the group were apparently out of the leader's acting range and a new leader was needed to handle them. For the 39 groups studied, "six of the ten leaders who performed tasks for which they had expressed preference maintained their leadership compared with only 10 of the 29 leaders who performed a task which they did not choose" (p. 41).

As Bavelas has said, "when specific situational patterns are different from organization to organization, one cannot say what personal traits will lead to acknowledged leadership" (10, p. 494). Gibb has stated, "a person does not become a leader by virtue of his possession of any one particular pattern of personality traits, but the pattern of personal characteristics of the leader must bear some relevant relationship to the present characteristics, activities, and goals of the group of which he is leader" (36, p. 889). Reviews of the literature by Stogdill (72) and Mann (59) deal exclusively with the personal factors associated with leadership. Based on these surveys, there is little meaningful connection between leadership and height and weight when considered for all types of groups. Among other factors, "fluency of speech, if not tone of voice, is a factor to be considered" (72, pp. 43–44), since it appears to facilitate communication; a person with this trait could well be chosen the leader if communication were of prime importance to the group. Kirscht, Lodahl, and Haire (57) had 22 three-person groups discuss a human relations case study for twenty minutes and then had them choose a representative (leader) from each group to discuss the same problem further with other representatives. It was found that "members who were chosen as representatives talked an average of 44.8% of the meeting time; non-representatives talked an average of 27.6% of the time" (p. 523). There was also a significant positive correlation between the person chosen as leader and the number of times he (a) gave suggestions, (b) asked for suggestions, and (c) gave orientation, as measured by interaction process analysis (see Chapter 4, Figure 2). Since the situation primarily involved discussion, not action, it is not surprising talkativeness was an important leadership variable.

Stogdill says, "it is very doubtful that leaders can be described with any degree of uniformity in terms of introversion-extroversion" (72, p. 49). Mann's study, based on about 13 papers written since 1948, also says that, "no single measure of extroversion is consistently related to leadership" (59, p. 249). One study which found extroversion relevant was conducted by Borg and Tupes (20) in an Air Force Officer Candidate School. Groups were formed, some of which discussed Air Force policy decisions while others solved "situational construction problems" (which involved getting out of a situation by constructing something). Personality ratings for all members showed that the significant traits relating to leadership were more socially oriented, like extroversion, than personally oriented, like orderliness of action—no doubt because social factors related more closely to the task performance than personal ones. Based on 12 studies, 9 since Stogdill's report that "leadership cannot be defined in terms of personal dominance" (72, p. 50), Mann concludes that "although the trend is not very strong, these data suggest that dominant or ascendent individuals have a greater chance of being designated leader" (p. 249). From nine studies, Mann states, "there is a slight positive association between masculinity and leadership" (p. 249), and from 17 studies, "in general there is a negative association between conservatism and leadership" (p. 250). Stogdill remarks that "studies do not lend convincing support to the view that leaders are necessarily persons who are characterized by a high degree of self-control" (72, p. 56). A "general trend . . . suggests that leaders rate higher than their followers in self-confidence and self-esteem" (72, p. 54). As an example of this finding, Beer, et al. (12) compared 10 leaders (men and women) of social groups on a school campus with 10 non-leaders from the groups.Their findings indicated the leaders rated higher in self-acceptance (self-confidence and self-esteem), need achievement (ambition), and interpersonal skills (such as warmth, tact, outgoingness). The relevant situation here is a social one demanding not dominance nor consideration of sheer physical size, but rather socially desirable traits. Then too, leaders are more aware "of how the group feels about them" than are non-leaders. Mann has reviewed 15 studies dealing with interpersonal sensitivity, the ability of a leader to guess his own status in a group as well as group opinions and attitudes. He finds there "appears to be a low but clearly positive relationship between interpersonal sensitivity and leadership" (59, p. 251). Chowdhry and Newcomb have stated, "other things equal, those members of a group will be most effective leaders who are most familiar with its standards, and most familiar with the degree to which those standards are shared by the group's members" (28, p. 51). They used several different groups each of which was to discuss a different social problem or issue. Prior to the discussion sessions, each person filled out an attitude questionnaire relating to the problem to be discussed. After the discussion, each group selected a leader. "It was found that leaders of a group are significantly superior to non-leaders . . . in their ability to judge group opinion on . . . relevant issues" (p. 56). Leaders, then, have a sensitivity to the group members. Bell and Hall (14) used 18 groups of four and five members each to discuss human relations problems. Each member was rated by every other member on his leadership and was also given an empathy test to measure the degree of correspondence between his feelings and attitudes and the group's. A small positive correlation between being selected as the leader and the empathy score seems to indicate that leaders perceive group feelings. Relating this leader sensitivity to the definition of a leader as influencer, Browne and Shore hypothesize, "the individual who will be most successful in influencing the actions of a group . . . will be the individual who knows the thinking of the group best" (22, p. 112). They attribute this prediction of attitudes to something they call "predictive abstracting"—"the process of selecting certain details from an event and eliminating other details which are included in the same event" (p. 112).

Stogdill indicates, "leaders are persons who tend to rate higher than average in popularity" (72, p. 59). Berkowitz (17) used 19 groups of six men each from an Air Force Officer Candidate School and, as part of their training, had them perform a simple bridge-building task requiring coordination of effort. Leadership nominations were made and a questionnaire about individual differences was filled out. "Individuals who received the greatest number of leadership nominations at the completion of the group task tended to have the following characteristics: (a) they frequently attempted to influence the behavior of the others . . . (b) they also were wanted as companions for a social evening" (p. 433). It is this latter factor that corresponds to popularity. Using four groups of men and women combined, to discuss social problems, Theodorson (76) found that group cohesiveness is an intervening variable between leadership and popularity, that is, its presence affected this relationship. Cohesiveness can be defined as the amount of attraction there is to the group (cf. Chapter 3). He found that, "under conditions of high cohesiveness leadership and popularity roles merge . . . the higher one is in the leadership hierarchy, the more popular he will be" (p. 59). Under such conditions, the group members will be strongly attracted to the group and, therefore, to the leader, the representative of the group. "Under conditions of low cohesiveness, leadership and popularity are segmentalized roles: being high in the leadership hierarchy does not necessarily mean high popularity" (76, p. 59).

A 1948 summary indicated the traits "with the highest over-all correlation with leadership are originality, popularity, sociability, judgment, aggressiveness, desire to excel, humor, cooperativeness, liveliness, and athletic ability, in approximate order of magnitude of average correlation coefficient" (72, p. 63). Given these relative characteristics, the important consideration now is the cause-effect relationship. As Gouldner has indicated, "trait studies usually do not discriminate between traits facilitating ascent to leadership and those enabling it to be maintained" (40, p. 24). Thus, a manifest trait may enable a person to be chosen as leader, but a latent trait may enable him to maintain the position. It is the situation the leader finds himself in that determines what traits need to be exhibited to maintain leadership. Furthermore, a significant correlation between two things does not by itself indicate anything about cause and effect—it merely indicates a degree of association. If, for a sample studied, a significant correlation is found between a particular trait and the person selected as leader, it is not possible to say without further analysis that the trait caused the person to be selected leader nor to say the fact of being leader caused the trait. It may be that the actual factor causing a person to be selected as leader is unknown, but it correlates with some common trait, say popularity, which in turn correlates with leadership. Of course, this unknown factor correlates with leadership indirectly since it is responsible for the popularity which results in leadership. In this type of situation, the trait (here, popularity) is known as an intervening variable; it looks as though it "causes" some effect when actually it does not. Another important, though less frequently occurring, problem concerns traits that arise by chance. If the researcher is operating at the 5% level, that is, he assumes 5% of the significant correlation coefficients to arise by chance alone, then correlations of 20 traits with leadership would produce one significant relationship just by chance. This "significant" finding would not occur if the study were performed again. Replication of trait-leadership experiments is thus an indispensable technique.

Fiedler (32, 33) has proposed a leadership-effectiveness trait that appears more independent of specific situations than the previously mentioned traits. He defines a leadership-effectiveness trait as "a consistent, reliably measurable personality attribute which differentiates effective from ineffective leaders" (32, p. 181). He points out that such a trait, like all the others, will be possessed to some degree by all members of a population but will be possessed most of the time by all effective leaders in all types of situations. The trait he suggests, the psychological distance between leader and the group, is measured by an Assumed Similarity between opposites (ASo) score on approximately 20 rating scales. The scales relate to such interpersonal dimensions as friendly-unfriendly, cooperative-uncooperative, confident-unsure, impatient-patient, responsible-undependable, etc. These 20 adjective pairs appear on a six point scale which the leader is asked to apply to his most preferred co-worker and his least preferred co-worker. The relationship or degree of correspondence between the leader's description of these two people (at opposite ends of the co-worker continuum) forms the ASo score. A low ASo score, i.e., a low "correlation" between his ratings for the two co-workers, indicates the leader is psychologically distant from the group as a whole. Conversely, a high ASo score means a high correspondence between his ratings for the two co-workers and indicates a relatively uncritical, i.e., psychologically imperceptive, acceptance of the group. For 14 high school basketball teams, using the number of games won as the effectiveness criterion, Fiedler (33) found a significant negative correlation between the ASo score of the team's leader and effectiveness—meaning the best teams had as their leaders boys who were psychologically distant from most of the players. For 22 student surveying teams composed of from three to four men, Fiedler found "good teams tended to choose relatively distant informal leaders" (33, p. 593), as was seen with the basketball teams. Similar negative correlations between the ASo score of the leader and the group's effectiveness were found for 53 B-29 bomber crews, 25 Army tank crews, groups in 16 work shifts of an open hearth steel mill, and groups in 32 small farmer-cooperative type organizations. These relationships hold when the leader is a leader as defined in this chapter, but do not necessarily hold when he is a leader only by virtue of his formal authority. Hutchins and Fiedler (52) used groups of 483 men in radar-tracking units and gun crews of the U. S. Air Defense Command in size from 6 to 17 men to further test the ASo-effectiveness findings. They found that "psychologically distant leaders will have better groups than will leaders who perceive similarity to their co-workers" (p. 394). An explanation of these consistent findings would be that leader control of the group is not possible when emotional ties (a psychologically close relationship) exist between leader and group members. If a leader "is emotionally dependent on another, he cannot afford to antagonize him since this might deprive him of the other man's support" (33, p. 596).

Leaders and Their Followers

Stogdill summarizes the trait approach by saying "a person does not become a leader by virtue of the possession of some combination of traits, but the pattern of personal characteristics of the leader must bear some relevant relationship to the characteristics, activities, and goals of the followers" (72, p. 64). As indicated earlier, the situation in which the leader finds himself *is* important. "Leadership is, then, to be understood as rather more than taking initiative, planning and organizing . . . leadership implies a particular dynamic relationship between the leader and his followers" (38, p. 227). Followers are important not only because individually they either accept or reject the leader, but because collectively they give him whatever power he may have. Therefore, as Sanford has indicated, "there is some justification for regarding the follower as the most crucial factor in any leadership event" (65, p. 4).

The leader brings to the task his needs and perceptual capacities, which are functions of his personality traits, the total situation, and the environment his followers create. Then, as Tannenbaum and Massarik (75) suggest, he seeks out those actions (usually in the form of influence attempts) which seem relevant to the goal he has in mind and coincide with his needs and perceptual capacities. The goal he chooses and his other actions, however, must also meet the needs of the group, the followers. Wolman (80) conducted an experiment with six college students trying to solve a problem. Four of the subjects were naïve, knowing nothing about the experiment, while the remaining two had full information. One of these persons was to act friendly yet appear incompetent in the task; the other was to act hostile and give help only when pressed hard, yet appear potentially competent. The need of the group was problem solution, and they chose as their informal leader the hostile person who appeared to possess the necessary information for problem solution. Wolman concluded the "results . . . seem to tie up leadership to the specific needs of the group" (pp. 22–23). In Greer's study (41) of Army Infantry rifle squads he found that when the leader satisfied his men's

needs, they performed better as a group. Thus the leader-follower relationship is not one-sided; "group members can often reciprocate a
leader's indulgences to them through effective performance" (41, p. 1),
thereby satisfying his need for success.

"In some circumstances the leader is an object for transference of
long-established feelings of dependence and submissiveness by followers"
(38, p. 904). This means group members who have the need to depend
upon others will seek as leader a person who will satisfy this need. If this
is the case, the leader derives his power and leadership status from
dependent persons. The influence of the leader can be, then, a function
of his follower's dependency feelings and his acceptance or rejection can
depend upon this fact. Sanford (66) had suggested using the authoritarian
dimension (measuring one's obedience to, and respect for, authority) as
a criterion for selecting followers. The rationale for this relates to the
dependency needs mentioned previously—the "authoritarian dimension"
merely provides a way of measuring them. The California F-scale is a
standardized test for measuring this authoritarian dimension: An F-plus
score on this test would represent the self-centered authoritarian personality,
and an F-minus score would represent the group-centered equalitarian
personality type. Haythorn, et al. (45) used several four-man groups to
solve human relations problems under the following conditions: (1) F-plus
leaders with F-plus followers, (2) F-plus leaders with F-minus followers,
(3) F-minus leaders with F-plus followers, (4) F-minus leaders with
F-minus followers. These researchers concluded that a conception of the
authoritarian dimension of the followers, the leaders, and the interaction
between the two was vital to any understanding of the total picture. Four
trained observers looking through a two-way mirror rated the working
groups on certain dimensions chosen by the experimenters. The "F-plus
leaders were rated as being less equalitarian, less concerned with group
approval, more autocratic, and less sensitive to others than F-minus
leaders . . . F-plus followers . . . were rated as being less equalitarian
behaviorally, and as showing less sensitivity to others" (p. 215) than
F-minus followers. These ratings are, essentially, in agreement with what
the F-scale purports to measure. It was found that "under F-minus leaders,
followers (either F-plus or F-minus) . . . would exert more influence on
group processes . . . would develop a less formal group structure" (p. 217).
Since these leaders were not autocratic, followers had more of an opportunity to contrtibute to and exert their influence upon the group. "Leaders
with F-minus followers would differ from those with F-plus followers by
(a) engaging in less autocratic behavior, and (b) being less distinct from
other group members" (p. 217)—by not "leading" too much. For groups
having leaders and followers with equivalent F-scale scores, "followers are
more secure . . . are more motivated to achieve the common group goal"

(p. 211) implying higher morale than in heterogenous F-scale score groups. In this situation, conflict of personalities, at least on the dimensions of the F-scale, between leader and followers would be eliminated, thereby creating a feeling of security and a willingness to work together. As Haythorn, *et al.* state, "the behavior of leaders is, to a significant degree a function of the attitudes or personality characteristics of the followers" (p. 218).

Hollander (50) has done an experiment with 187 naval aviation cadets that indicated those chosen as followers were also chosen as leaders. After their graduation from a sixteen-week training course, the cadets were asked to assume they were going on some undisclosed mission together. Each of them was asked to: (1) list 3 cadets they believed were most, and 3 cadets least, qualified to lead; (2) list 3 cadets he most wanted, and 3 cadets he least wanted to follow in his group, and (3) list the 3 cadets who were his best friends. In listing these men, the cadets were to assume that any abilities they thought important, were; that is, each cadet defined leadership in his own terms. The correlation between leadership and friendship was .47, between followship and friendship .55, and between leadership and followership .92. The first two correlations indicated that those chosen as leaders and those chosen as followers were not always the ones chosen as friends. The high leadership-followship correlation indicates there is little difference personality-wise between leaders and followers. The author also reports an unpublished study by Kubany on 87 medical school seniors showing a correlation of .85 between those the seniors would choose as a family doctor (leader) and those they would choose to turn their practice over to (follower). It may be that a leader will choose as his followers those who are also leaders with the expectation that they will help him with the leadership position.

Bass (5) has indicated it is sometimes difficult to determine just who is leading and who is following. The behavior of a follower can often effect the behavior of the leader so that he has to make behavioral adjustments to the follower's demands. Furthermore, if two people in interaction are observed, "the question as to who is leading and who is following may depend on whose actions we observe first" (5, p. 94). If a leader-follower difference does not exist, and rather than one depending upon the other for need satisfaction, there is a mutual dependency and sharing of the task at hand, then the notion of leadership has no long-term meaning relevant to one person.

Leadership Roles and Functions

As indicated previously, the trait approach to leadership generally breaks down when the context of the leadership changes. As Gouldner (40, p. 32) has said, the "hypothesis that there are some traits common to all leaders is presently unfashionable." Rather, he says, "leadership is . . . a role which an individual occupies at a given time in a given group" (p. 20). Thus, the person doing the correct thing at the correct time becomes the leader. Bavelas has said, "almost any member of a group may become its leader under circumstances that enable him to perform the required functions of leadership" (10, p. 494). The function may be conceptually simple, such as choosing the group goal, supervising performance, making decisions, planning, etc.; or it may be rather complex, such as serving as the group's ego. Schutz has pointed out that, "the leadership functions in the small group are the same as the ego functions within an individual personality" (68, p. 48); that is to say, the leader in some way integrates the group's needs with reality. The ego develops by integrating *outer reality* (the restrictions of the real world), *interpersonal needs* and a *conflict-free sphere* (consisting of such things as intelligence and talent) for the individual (68). "If a leader can enable the group to perform all the functions needed to integrate these three spheres, he will have done all that is required of him" (p. 56), and could easily be chosen leader.

FIRO (Fundamental Interpersonal Relations Orientation) theory, as developed by Schutz, states "there are three fundamental interpersonal needs—*inclusion, control,* and *affection*—and in order for an individual (or group) to function optimally he must establish and maintain a satisfactory relation in all three areas" (p. 57). Inclusion is the amount of contact or interaction with people or things; control refers to control over the social environment; affection is a feeling of social "closeness." Beyond this, the needs must be integrated with outer reality and the conflict-free sphere. The leader serves as the completer of any of these functions the group does not perform. "This conception also implies that when the group is fulfilling all its functions adequately, the most appropriate behavior for the leader is inaction" (p. 62).

In many situations, the function of the leader is to influence members of the group to pursue certain activities beneficial to the group. The amount of influence available is, according to Gibb (39), affected by *role boundaries, role repertoire,* and *role consonance.* Role boundary refers to "the boundary that encompasses the member acts the group will accept from the individual" (p. 68). Certain acts are considered acceptable to the group's standards, while others are not. The role repertoire refers to "the range and adequacy of the role behaviors" (p. 73) that are available for use by an individual or group. Role consonance is the harmony of the behavior with the "group goal system" (p. 75). All of this would imply that the influence for any group member would be at its greatest when the influence acts were within the acceptable sphere of behavior (role boundary), somewhat diverse (role repertoire), and in agreement with group goals (role consonance). On the basis of laboratory experiments upon college students and observations of adult human relations training sessions, Gibb (39) has shown that these three determinants of influence potential correlate negatively with defensive behavior in the group. Defensive behavior can be considered as aggression or withdrawal of a person brought on by "an individual need to preserve a stable perception of the self or to defend the self from perceived attack" (p. 67). Thus, the greater the defensive atmosphere in a group, the less the influence possibilities because of reduced role consonance and a more limited role repertoire and boundary. In being defensive, a person restricts his acceptance of other people's behaviors and is more concerned with personal, rather than group goals. If the role of a leader is to influence, then it is also to decrease defensive behavior within the group to perform this function.

To indicate there is but one role, or set of behaviors a leader performs, is to limit his function for the group. As was previously mentioned, a more general set of roles for the leader could be to act as completer for the group—this would involve several different role-playing activities. Benne and Sheats (15) have indicated "leadership functions can be defined in terms of facilitating identification, acceptance, development and allocation of group required roles" (p. 42). These group required roles are group task (selection, definition, and solution of problems); group building and maintenance, (developing and preserving the group); individual roles (satisfying individual needs). A further breakdown of the roles is also possible; for example, within the "group task" classification are twelve available roles (pp. 43–44): (1) *initiator-contributor*; (2) *information seeker*; (3) *opinion seeker*; (4) *information giver*; (5) *opinion giver*; (6) *elaborator*; (7) *coordinator*; (8) *orienter,* with respect to group goals; (9) *evaluator-critic*; (10) *energizer,* who "prods groups to action"; (11) *procedural technician* who does routine "housekeeping" tasks for the group; and (12) *recorder.* These roles, or most of them, have to be played by someone, either the leader or the members, but, as indicated, the leader is responsible for providing the environment in which the roles can exist and be fulfilled. Within the "group building and maintenance" classification there are seven roles (pp. 44–45): (1) the *encourager*; (2) the *harmonizer,* who reconciles disagreements; (3) the *compromiser,* who admits his errors; (4) *gate keeper and expediter,* who keeps communication channels open; (5) *standard setter*; (6) the *group observer and commentator* who gives feedback of the group's actions; and (7) *follower.* These activities are quite different from the previous set, as are the individual roles from either of these categories. Benne and Sheats have listed eight individual activities or roles that can be taken to satisfy individual needs (pp. 45–46): (1) the *aggressor,* who attacks the group or the problem it is working on; (2) the *blocker,* who is resistant and negative; (3) *recognition seeker*; (4) *self-*

confessor, who provides subjective feelings, insights, and intuition; (5) the *playboy,* who has a lack of involvement in group's process; (6) *dominator,* who asserts authority; (7) *help-seeker,* seeking comfort from the group; and (8) the *special interest pleader,* who speaks for a particular subgroup. Not all of the three sets of roles will emerge in a group, nor will one person necessarily be restricted to a single role. But the significant thing is that the possible roles for three main situations groups find themselves in are clearly listed; some group members may naturally emerge in a particular role or roles, others may have to be assigned a role. With the given situation determining what roles are legitimate, the leader can develop, assign, and maintain the appropriate roles. The choice of leader, however, depends on the situation—personality traits exhibited in one situation would not be necessarily relevant in another situation.

When People Attempt to Lead

An important concern of leadership study is why people attempt to lead. Inextricably tied up with this question is why people attempt to join a group or remain in it in the first place (this aspect has been discussed in the chapter on group cohesiveness). The answer to both questions is that they expect some reward or return as a result of participation. Some will be satisfied "if and when the group attains task success; other members will be satisfied mainly if the group affords opportunity to interact harmoniously with others; still others will be primarily attracted to the group if they expect to gain esteem status and other direct rewards" (5, pp. 148–149).

Hemphill (47) has performed a series of experiments, using male students, to answer the question of when people will attempt leadership acts, that is, to consider under what conditions people will be encouraged to lead. He found the "why" of leading to be associated with the rewards gained and the "when" to be related to "expectations that the group task can be accomplished, . . . specific task requirements . . . which create requirements for someone to lead, and . . . personal acceptance by their fellow group members which comes about as a result of attempts to lead" (p. 211). Thus, when an obtainable goal exists, when leadership is needed and there is encouragement for it, and when rewards for goal attainment are extant, people will attempt to lead. Furthermore, other reasons, though less strong, are "possession of task-relevant information not readily trans-mittable to others, and . . . previously acquired leadership status in the group" (p. 211). If a group member is obviously competent in a relevant area and "if other group members are aware of his expert knowledge, he encounters great pressure to lead . . . he is expected to make recommendations for courses of action" (p. 212). Hemphill found that a person who was the leader on one task because he possessed task-relevant information was also likely to be selected as the leader on a second task even if he had no relevant information. In other words, his leadership status carried over from one task to another—the condition was right for his leadership bid.

Bass, et al. (8) used five-person groups of R.O.T.C. cadets to relate leadership to control and group motivational factors. There were three different motivational categories into which the groups fell: high motivation to continue on with advanced R.O.T.C. training, medium, and low. Within these categories, different amounts of control ("the ability to reward or punish other members") were given to various group members in a problem-solving task. It was found that "a member's attempted leadership is higher, the higher his control and the higher the group's motivation" (p. 358). When a group is motivated to reach a goal, and one of the group members possesses a certain amount of control, then conditions exist for that person to attempt to lead. Schlesinger, Jackson and Butman (67) studied the effects of control on 23 committees composed of 106 middle-management personnel in a large utility company. Each of the managers was rated as being either a high or low control person; then the experimenters manipulated the chairmanships of the committees, unknown to the committee, to obtain both high and low control chairmen. The researchers found that the high control chairmen were seen by the committee members as contributing more and being more skillful chairmen. It also appeared that exerting this high control did not decrease the amount of inter-personal friendliness in the group (p. 362). However, "when the participants do not perceive the designated leader as satisfactorily performing the controlling functions, the participants increase their own attempts to influence their fellow members" (p. 363). Control is a two-edged sword that either makes a leader or brings on his demise through the emergence of new leaders.

Conferences in 72 business and government organizations were observed by Crockett (30) to determine the conditions under which emergent leaders, as opposed to appointed leaders, arise. The observations indicated "emergent leaders will occur more often in groups where the official leader does not perform the leadership functions" (p. 378). The results of Schlesinger, et al. (67) corroborate those of Crockett.

Crockett also found "emergent leaders will be found more often in groups where divergent interests are present" (p. 378) as the formal leader probably would not have the time to deal with the problem. Characteristics of these emergent leaders were that they were above the median level of the other members in their rank (status), expertness, and self-oriented needs; they had a high stake in the outcome of the meetings and the group felt it needed them more than some other members (p. 382). These are, in fact, the usual leadership traits. Carter, *et al.* (25), in studying 10 groups of 4 Naval R.O.T.C. cadets engaged in discussion, reasoning, and mechanical assembly tasks, found a definite difference in the behavior of emergent leaders as opposed to appointed leaders. Some of the group meetings had an emergent leader, the others had leaders appointed by the researchers. During the meetings, the group leader and the members were rated on 53 behavioral categories by observers through a two-way mirror. The researchers inferred from the data that "the appointed leader conceives his role as one of coordinator rather than as a director or controller of the group's activities" (p. 518). Directing or controlling a group, rather than coordinating it, requires more aggressive behavior—behavior an appointed leader probably is not immediately capable of giving. Borg (19) even found "the performance of designated leaders (other than the emergent leader) is not significantly different than the individual's performance when he is not designated leader" (p. 102). In using 14 groups of Air Force Officer Candidate School men with no clear leader in a series of training problems, he found the "over-all performance of teams in which no leader emerged is significantly inferior to the performance of teams in which one leader has emerged" (p. 102). He points out that the "presence of a leader increases leadership performance of followers rather than suppressing such performance" (p. 102), but where two leaders emerge, the followers suppress leadership acts, apparently because the two leaders monopolize the situation. A group needs a leader if it is to reach its goal; therefore, certain minimal conditions for leadership are necessary to encourage the emergence of a leader.

Leadership Under Stress

The "distinctive element in stress is . . . the lack of structure . . . in reality experienced by the individual or group as a result" (77, p. 101) of the stressful situation. The stress or crisis produces a new situation to which the group does not know how to respond. As indicated, when a leader does not perform his proper function of, say, controlling a group, other leaders who can will emerge. When there is no leader initially, "whoever is able and willing to provide the essential structure emerges as leader" (77, p. 101); the situation determines who the leader shall be. However, the results of research Torrance has done with military groups indicates "the leader of a small group under stress should be a regular member of the group and should be the same as the official leader under normal conditions" (77, p. 110). Under these conditions, the leader has more influence over the group's behavior. Regardless of who the leader is, though, under stress, "leaders appear to feel a greater than usual need to seek the judgments of group members when conditions become stressful" (p. 114); the situation is difficult and help is needed. Hamblin (43) produced stressful situations for adult men and women playing a shuffleboard type game to see how leadership was affected. The game was played according to certain rules the players had to discover as they played—a red light that went on meant a rule was violated, a green light meant the proper rule had been used. The subjects were to be ego-involved in the game by telling them how well high school students performed, thus making the adults want to do the task better. Crisis was introduced to some of the groups by changing the rules of the game in such a way the players could never really do as well as the high school groups. For the crisis groups, the "regular" leader (as judged by certain behaviors) was replaced in 9 out of 12 groups, as compared to replacement in only 3 out of 12 groups when no crisis was introduced. The regular leaders could not handle the changed situation because they were not trained for working under stress. Such training to retain the regular leadership would be desirable as inferred from the findings of Torrance (77).

Bass (5) points out that many kinds of studies both in the laboratory and "the real world" indicate the "validity of the theorems that (1) leadership acts during crises are likely to be immediately effective if they are made quickly, and (2) attempts to coerce or persuade are more likely to be successful during crises than when no emergencies exist" (p. 439). A crisis by its very nature requires fast action and this is immediately perceived as good action. In time, of course, if it is obvious to the group that all the leader's actions are producing heat but no light, he will be replaced. Since the group realizes action is necessary, they will more readily respond to the leader's coercive acts in a time of crisis than in ordinary conditions.

Communication and Leadership

If the leader is one who influences others, then he must communicate rather well with them. It is not surprising that in communication nets, the leader is most likely to be in the centralmost position, because this is the most influential position. As Bavelas has stated "the individual occupying the most central position in a pattern was most likely to be recognized as the leader" (9, p. 676). Shaw (70), in his experiments has also considered the leader to be the person in the center of the communication net.

Leaders may want to influence group attitudes or to initiate action from the group. Back (3) proposes a different pattern of communication for each of the above purposes. If the leader wishes to influence the group's attitudes, his communication should be highly redundant, stressing a few points over and over again in a different manner (form is varied, content is redundant). If the leader wants action from the group, he should try to get across several points using the same communication technique (form is constant, content is high in information). Back is claiming attitude change can be effected by presenting the new information to affect attitudes in many different ways so that there is little chance of the recipient missing the message content. To initiate group action, the leader presents several different reasons for action so that at least one of them will initiate the action. Of course, both action and attitudes will be affected if the form and content are redundant, for then "communication becomes a ritual . . . uniting a great number of people in common beliefs and common actions" (p. 148).

As the size of a group changes, the perceptions of the leader by the group members also change. Hemphill (46) had 365 college students and adults fill out questionnaires about leaders they had known, regardless of the kind of group. He found "there is a tendency for the leadership role in the larger groups to take on a greater degree of impersonal direction connected with firmness and impartiality in enforcement of rules" (p. 19). A larger group requires more total communication acts of the leader to maintain the same degree of group-centeredness than does a small group. It is not surprising that for larger groups the leader most often has to limit these acts and concentrate on such other matters as group maintenance and goal attainment. Medalia found for 50 squadrons of the Air Defense Command that as unit "size increases, median perception of leader's human relations mindedness decreases" (60, p. 65), where human relations mindedness means an "emphasis on obtaining the voluntary cooperation of followers" (p. 65). An explanation the author offers is that the groups *expect* the leader to be human relations minded (group-centered) with small groups so this is what they perceive; even though a leader of a large group may behave as he would with a smaller unit, members do not expect group-centered behavior and, hence, do not perceive it.

Leader Assessment

It is, of course, desirable to assess a leader's performance to determine whether or not he is doing the job required of him by his superiors or by his group. If his function is goal attainment, then the time required to reach the goal becomes a criterion with which to measure leadership effectiveness. If it is to keep the group needs satisfied, then a poll of individual attitudes would answer the leadership effectiveness question. If the leader's function is to engage in certain behaviors, then a comparison of these desired behaviors with the actual ones yields an assessment. The Leader Behavior Description Questionnaire developed at Ohio State (48) lists ten dimensions related to leadership behavior: initiation (originates ideas), membership (interacts with group), representation (acts for the group), integration (adapts group to individuals and vice versa), organization (structures relationships), domination (restricts behavior), communication (exchange of information both up and down levels), recognition (approval or disapproval of behavior), and production (develop greater work effort). There are probably as many leader behavior checklists as there are concepts of leadership; but this is reasonable since the assessment concern may be only with a very specific aspect of leadership.

While leadership is usually assessed over a past period of time, it is sometimes desirable to apply assessment to the future—that is, to predict potential leadership effectiveness. The leaderless group discussion (LGD) offers one way of doing this. In this situation, a leaderless group is formed to discuss some problem, and each member is evaluated on his leadership "abilities" by researchers. Then, this leadership score is correlated with his leadership performance in a real-life situation. If the correlation is significantly high, the leaderless group discussion technique may serve as a predictor of future leadership abilities. Of course, the LGD will predict best when the session's task is equivalent to the real-world task, i.e., the high correlation is predetermined. Of course, adoption of a leadership trait approach would eliminate this problem automatically.

Bass, Klubeck, and Wurster have stated that "a substantial body of evidence is available to suggest that behavior in the initially leaderless group discussion is indicative of leadership potential for a fairly wide range of situations" (7, p. 26). In a review article on the subject (4), Bass lists those groups which have successfully been used in LGD experiments; R.O.T.C. students, sorority and fraternity members, foremen, supervisors, etc. Kiessling and Kalish (56) used 87 applicants for the Honolulu Police Academy and after putting them in groups, gave them a "police problem" to discuss. A significant relationship was found between success in the LGD and actual scores on a police aptitude test. It does appear, then, that the leaderless group discussion technique has predictive validity, but its administration takes time, and so the question arises, could this time be used to predict future leadership capabilities more accurately by another, less time-consuming method?

Leadership Styles

The leader, as director or influencer of the group, has at his disposal several means for directing the activities of the group. Knickerbocker (58, p. 39) lists four methods: force, paternalism (developing the loyalty and gratitude of followers for leader), bargain (certain satisfactions would be supplied the followers in return for the leadership position), and mutual means (having the same objectives as group). Consideration of the situation, the followers, and the personality of the leader would determine which approach would be the most successful. Relevant to these methods of influence is the leadership style, the way in which the leader chooses to "lead." Five main leadership styles have been defined: authoritarian, democratic, laissez-faire, bureaucratic, and charismatic. The first three were proposed by White and Lippitt (78) and the latter two by Bonner (18). In the authoritarian style "all determination of policy [is] by the leader" (78, p. 528); this style is most effectively used where firm control is necessary. In the democratic style, "policies [are] a matter of group discussion and decision" (78, p. 528); this style is applicable in the bargain situation of Knickerbocker. For the mutual means situation, the laissez-faire style is best, as it offers "complete freedom for group or individual decision" (78, p. 258); if there is agreement between leader and followers on goals, then little leadership is necessary. Influencing by means of paternalism could be accomplished by any of these leadership styles, since followers become obligated on an individual rather than a group basis. Bureaucratic leadership refers generally to the leadership exhibited by someone occupying a bureaucratic office (supervision in this book's terms); a combination of the three above styles would typify it. Charismatic leadership is leadership based on "supernatural" or spiritual qualities that emotionally attract followers—qualities that Joan of Arc, for instance, possessed.

White and Lippitt (78) studied the effects of the authoritarian, democratic, and laissez-faire leadership styles on groups of ten-year-old boys. They rotated the adult leaders of four groups of five boys' hobby clubs every six weeks so that each club experienced each leadership style with a different leader. "The groups were roughly equated on patterns of interpersonal relationships, intellectual, physical, and socio-economic status, and personality characteristics" (p. 527), so that one group's response to leadership would be expected to be similar to another's. The purpose of these clubs was, of course, recreational, but this did not prevent evaluation in terms of social goals (recreation) and work goals (hobby goals). As expected, the most work was done under autocracy because of the greater pressure, and the least work was done under laissez-faire, the condition of least pressure to produce. In terms of the social goals, there is "no reason to think that democracy is necessarily superior from the standpoint of immediate personal satisfaction . . . autocracy is often satisfying to some of the needs, in passivity . . . in not having to think" (p. 543). Generally, however, autocracy is "frustrating insofar as it imposes barriers to the satisfaction of individual needs" (p. 543) and can lead to hostility and aggression. As for interpersonal relationships, "there was more group-mindedness and more friendliness in democracy" (p. 546).

Baumgartel (11) has conducted a similar investigation of leadership styles in the research laboratories of a large research organization. Of the 20 labs studied, 6 had directors operating in a laissez-faire style, 7 were participatory (democratic), and 5 were directive (autocratic); the other two did not fit neatly into the other categories. Questionnaires were given the scientists in the laboratories, asking about the leadership climate developed by the research directors whose duty it was to direct and formulate the research programs. For the participatory climate, as compared with the other two, there was greater over-all satisfaction with organizational leadership, a higher feeling of research orientation and freedom of originality, and a greater sense of progress toward research goals (p. 359). The directive leadership style generally had the worst ratings on these variables of satisfaction, orientation, etc. This probably had to do with the fact that research scientists do not enjoy being passive; thus, this study, contrasted with White and Lippitt's, reveals that groups of differing composition may react variously to the same kind of leadership. As with the boys, though, "directive leadership often creates suppressed resentments and hostilities which impair performance and diminish satisfaction" (p. 353).

The various leadership styles have their unique effects on the group regardless of whether the group has elected the leader or has merely accepted his supervision. Actually, the two above-mentioned studies relate to supervision, since the "leader" is not chosen by the group, but is self-appointed or chosen by superiors. Under real leadership, however, the dissatisfaction resulting from an autocratic approach would lead to a change of leadership.

Leadership style or supervisory style has been a concern of educators, also, who would like to know the effects upon attitudes and learning. With regard to the former, Hare (44, p. 317) concludes from a consideration of over 10 studies that "task-centered, demanding teachers were found to elicit from students hostility, apathy, and other signs of withdrawal, whereas accepting student-supportive teachers decreased anxiety and produced greater interaction." These findings are similar to those in studies of autocratic versus democratic leadership; the findings of White and Lippitt and Page and McGinnies (62) concur. The actual effect of different kinds of leadership on learning seems to be negligible: "Little difference has been found when students from both types of classes are given the same examination" (44, p. 317). Nachman and Opachinsky (61) and Feldhusen (31) report that for psychology classes, there is no significant difference in the subject matter learned (based on examinations) between students in large classes and those in small ones, indicating that any feelings of "closeness" in smaller groups are not important in learning.

Leadership style, in one way or another, does affect a variety of groups in different situations.

LEADERSHIP REFERENCES

1. Argyris, Chris. Organizational leadership. In *Leadership and Interpersonal Behavior*, Luigi Petrullo and Bernard M. Bass (eds.). New York: Holt, Rinehart & Winston, Inc., 1961.

2. Asch, M. J. Nondirective teaching in psychology: an experimental study. *Psychological Monographs* 1951, 65, No. 4, Whole No. 321.

3. Back, Kurt W. Power, influence and pattern of communication. In *Leadership and Interpersonal Behavior*, Luigi Petrullo and Bernard M. Bass (eds.). New York: Holt, Rinehart & Winston, Inc., 1961.

4. Bass, Bernard M. The leaderless group discussion. *Psychological Bulletin* 1954, 51, 465–492.

5. ———. *Leadership, Psychology and Organizational Behavior*. New York: Harper & Row, Publishers, 1960.

6. ——— and Norton, Fay-Tyler M. Group size and leaderless discussions. *Journal of Applied Psychology* 1951, 35, 397–400.

7. ———; Klubeck, Stanley and Wurster, Cecil R. Factors influencing reliability and validity of leaderless group discussion assessment. *Journal of Applied Psychology* 1953, 37, 26–30.

8. ———; Pryer, Margaret W.; Gaier, Eugene L. and Flint, Austin W. Interacting effects of control, motivation, group practice, and problem difficulty on attempted leadership. *Journal of Abnormal and Social Psychology* 1958, 56, 352–358.

9. Bavelas, Alex. Communication patterns in task-oriented groups. In *Group Dynamics*, Dorwin Cartwright and Alvin Zander (eds.). Evanston, Ill.: Row, Peterson & Company, 1960. (Also in *Journal of the Acoustical Society of America* 1950, 22, 725–730.)

10. ———. Leadership: man and function. *Administrative Science Quarterly* 1960, 4, 491–498.

11. Baumgartel, Howard. Leadership style as a variable in research administration. *Administrative Science Quarterly* 1957, 2, 344–360.

12. Beer, Michael; Buckhout, Robert; Horowitz, Milton W. and Levy, Seymour. Some perceived properties of the difference between leaders and non-leaders. *The Journal of Psychology* 1959, 47, 49–56.

13. Bell, Graham B. and French, Robert L. Consistency of individual leadership position in small groups of varying membership. *Journal of Abnormal and Social Psychology* 1950, 45, 764–767.

14. ——— and Hall, Harry E., Jr. The relationship between leadership and empathy. *Journal of Abnormal and Social Psychology* 1954, 49, 156–157.

15. Benne, Kenneth D. and Sheats, Paul. Functional roles of group members. *Journal of Social Issues* 1948, 4(2), 41–49.

16. Bennis, Warren G. Leadership theory and administrative behavior. *Administrative Science Quarterly* 1959, 4, 259–301.

17. Berkowitz, Leonard. Social desirability and frequency of influence attempts as factors in leadership choice. *Journal of Personality* 1956, 24, 424–435.

18. Bonner, Hubert. *Group Dynamics.* New York: The Ronald Press Company, 1959.

19. Borg, Walter R. The behavior of emergent and designated leaders in situational tests. *Sociometry* 1957, 20, 95–104.

20. —— and Tupes, Ernst C. Personality characteristics related to leadership behavior in two types of small group situational problems. *Journal of Applied Psychology* 1958, 42, 252–256.

21. Borgatta, Edgar F.; Bales, Robert F. and Couch, Arthur S. Some findings relevant to the great man theory of leadership. *American Sociological Review* 1954, 19, 755–759.

22. Browne, C. G. and Shore, Richard P. Leadership and predictive abstracting. *Journal of Applied Psychology* 1956, 40, 112–116.

23. Carter, Launor. Some research on leadership in small groups. In *Groups, Leadership and Men*, by Harold Guetzkow (ed.). Pittsburgh: Carnegie Press, 1951.

24. ——; Haythorn, William and Howell, Margaret. A further investigation of the criteria of leadership. *Journal of Abnormal and Social Psychology* 1950, 45, 350–358.

25. ——; Shriver, Beatrice and Lanzetta, John. The behavior of leaders and other group members. In *Group Dynamics,* Dorwin Cartwright and Alvin Zander (eds.). Evanston, Ill.: Row, Peterson & Company, 1960. (Also in *Journal of Abnormal and Social Psychology* 1950, 46, 589–595).

26. Cartwright, Dorwin and Zander, Alvin (eds.). *Group Dynamics.* Evanston, Ill.: Row, Peterson & Company, 1960.

27. Cattell, Raymond B. New concepts for measuring leadership in terms of group syntality. *Human Relations* 1951, 4, 161–184.

28. Chowdhry, Kamla and Newcomb, Theodore M. The relative abilities of leaders and non-leaders to estimate opinions of their own groups. *Journal of Abnormal and Social Psychology* 1952, 47, 51–57.

29. Cowley, W. H. The traits of face-to-face leaders. *Journal of Abnormal and Social Psychology* 1931, 26, 304–313.

30. Crockett, Walter H. Emergent leadership in small, decision-making groups. *Journal of Abnormal and Social Psychology* 1955, 51, 378–383.

31. Feldhusen, John F. The effects of small and large group instruction on learning of subject matter, attitudes and interests. *The Journal of Psychology* 1963, 55, 357–362.

32. Fiedler, Fred E. Leadership and leadership effectiveness traits: a reconceptualization of the leadership trait problem. In *Leadership and Interpersonal Behavior,* Luigi Petrullo and Bernard M. Bass (eds.). New York: Holt, Rinehart & Winston, Inc., 1961.

33. ——. The leader's psychological distance and group effectiveness. In *Group Dynamics,* Dorwin Cartwright and Alvin Zander (eds.). Evanston, Ill.: Row, Peterson & Company, 1960.

34. Fox, William M. Group reaction to two types of conference leadership. *Human Relations* 1957, 10, 279–288.

35. French, John R. P. and Rawen, Bertram. The bases of social power. In *Group Dynamics,* Dorwin Cartwright and Alvin Zander (eds.). Evanston, Ill.: Row, Peterson & Company, 1960.

36. Gibb, Cecil A. Leadership. In *Handbook of Social Psychology,* Gardner Lindzey (ed.). Cambridge, Mass.: Addison-Wesley Publishing Co., Inc., 1954.

37. ——. The principles and traits of leadership. *Journal of Abnormal and Social Psychology* 1947, 42, 267–284.

38. ——. The sociometry of leadership in temporary groups. *Sociometry* 1950, 13, 226–243.

39. Gibb, Jack R. Defense level and influence potential in small groups. In *Leadership and Interpersonal Behavior,* Luigi Petrullo and Bernard M. Bass (eds.). New York: Holt, Rinehart & Winston, Inc., 1961.

40. Gouldner, A. W. (ed.) *Studies in Leadership.* New York: Harper & Row, Publishers, 1950.

41. Greer, F. Loyal. Leader indulgence and group performance. *Psychological Monographs* 1961, 75, No. 12, Whole No. 516.

42. Halpin, Andrew W. The leadership behavior and combat performance of airplane commanders. *Journal of Abnormal and Social Psychology* 1954, 49, 19–22.

43. Hamblin, Robert L. Leadership and crises. In *Group Dynamics* Dorwin Cartwright and Alvin Zander (eds.). Evanston, Ill.: Row, Peterson & Company, 1960. (Also in *Sociometry* 1958, 21, 322–335.)

44. Hare, A. Paul. *Handbook of Small Group Research.* New York: Free Press of Glencoe, Inc., 1962.

45. Haythorn, William; Couch, Arthur; Haefner, Don; Langham, Peter and Carter, Launor. The effects of varying combinations of authoritarian and equalitarian leaders and followers. *Journal of Abnormal and Social Psychology* 1956, 53, 210–219.

46. Hemphill, John K. Relations between the size of the group and the behavior of "superior" leaders. *The Journal of Social Psychology* 1950, 32, 11–22.

47. ——. Why people attempt to lead. In *Leadership and Interpersonal Behavior,* Luigi Petrullo and Bernard M. Bass (eds.). New York: Holt, Rinehart & Winston, Inc., 1961.

48. —— and Coons, Alvin E. Development of the leader behavior description questionnaire. In *Leader Behavior: Its Description and Measurement,* Ralph M. Stogdill and Alvin E. Coons (eds.). Columbus, Ohio: Ohio State University, Bureau of Business Research, Monograph No. 88, 1957.

49. ——; Pepinsky, Pauline N.; Shevitz, Reuben N.; Jaynes, William E. and Christner, Charlotte A. The relation between possession of task-relevant information and attempts to lead. *Psychological Monographs* 1956, 70, No. 7, Whole No. 414.

50. Hollander, E. P. Emergent leadership and social influence. In *Leadership and Interpersonal Behavior,* Luigi Petrullo and Bernard M. Bass (eds.). New York: Holt, Rinehart & Winston, Inc., 1961.

51. Homans, George C. *The Human Group.* New York: Harcourt, Brace & World, Inc., 1950.

52. Hutchins, Edwin B. and Fieldler, Fred E. Task-oriented and quasi-therapeutic role functions of the leader in small military groups. *Sociometry* 1960, 23, 393–406.

53. Jenkins, William O. A review of leadership studies with particular reference to military problems. *Psychological Bulletin* 1947, 44, 54–79.

54. Kaess, Walter A.; Witryol, Sam L. and Nolan, Richard E. Reliability, sex differences and validity in the leaderless group discussion technique. *Journal of Applied Psychology* 1961, 45, 345–350.

55. Katz, Elihu; Blau, Peter M.; Brown, Morton L. and Strodtbeck, Fred L. Leadership stability and social change: an experiment with small groups. *Sociometry* 1957, 20, 36–50.

56. Kiessling, Ralph J. and Kalish, Richard A. Correlates of success in leaderless group discussion. *The Journal of Social Psychology* 1961, 54, 359–365.

57. Kirscht, John P.; Lodahl, Thomas M. and Haire, Mason. Some factors in the selection of leaders by members of small groups. In *Group Dynamics,* Dorwin Cartwright and Alvin Zander (eds.). Evanston, Ill.: Row, Peterson & Company, 1960. (Also in *Journal of Abnormal and Social Psychology* 1959, 58, 406–408.)

58. Knickerbocker, Irving. Leadership: a conception and some implications. *The Journal of Social Issues* 1948, 4(3), 23–40.

59. Mann, R. D. A review of the relationships between personality and performance in small groups. *Psychological Bulletin* 1959, 56, 241–270.

60. Medalia, Nahum Z. Unit size and leadership perception. *Sociometry* 1954, 17, 64–67.

61. Nachman, M. and Opachinsky, S. The effects of different teaching methods: a methodological study. *Journal of Educational Psychology* 1958, 49, 245–249.

62. Page, Richard H. and McGinnies, Elliott. Comparison of two styles of leadership in small group discussion. *Journal of Applied Psychology* 1959, 43, 240–245.

63. Petrullo, Luigi and Bass, Bernard M. (eds.). *Leadership and Interpersonal Behavior.* New York: Holt, Rinehart & Winston, Inc., 1961.

64. Pryer, Margaret W.; Flint, Austin W. and Bass, Bernard M. Group effectiveness and consistency of leadership. *Sociometry* 1962, 25, 391–397.

65. Sanford, Fillmore H. *Authoritarianism and Leadership.* Philadelphia: Institute for Research in Human Relations, 1950.

66. ———. Leadership identification and acceptance. In *Groups, Leadership and Men,* Harold Guetzkow (ed.). Pittsburgh: Carnegie Press, 1951.

67. Schlesinger, Laurence; Jackson, Jay M. and Butman, Jean. Leader-member interaction in management committees. *Journal of Abnormal and Social Psychology* 1960, 61, 360–364.

68. Schutz, William C. The ego, FIRO theory and the leader as completer. In *Leadership and Interpersonal Behavior,* Luigi Petrullo and Bernard M. Bass (eds.) New York: Holt, Rinehart & Winston, Inc. 1961.

69. Shartle, Carroll L. Studies in naval leadership. Part I. In *Groups, Leadership and Men,* Harold Guetzkow (ed.). Pittsburgh: Carnegie Press, 1951.

70. Shaw, Marvin E. A comparison of two types of leadership in various communication nets. *Journal of Abnormal and Social Psychology* 1955, 50, 127–134.

71. Stogdill, Ralph M. Leadership, membership and organization. *Psychological Bulletin* 1950, 47, 1–14.

72. ———. Personal factors associated with leadership: a survey of the literature. *Journal of Psychology* 1948, 25, 35–71.

73. ———. Studies in naval leadership. Part II. In *Groups, Leadership and Men,* Harold Guetzkow (ed.). Pittsburgh: Carnegie Press, 1951.

74. ——— and Coons, Alvin E. (eds.). *Leadership Behavior: Its Description and Measurement.* Columbus, Ohio: Ohio State University, Bureau of Business Research, Monograph No. 88, 1957.

75. Tannenbaum, Robert and Massarik, Fred. Leadership: a frame of reference. *Management Science* 1957, 4, 1–19.

76. Theodorson, George A. The relationship between leadership and popularity roles in small groups. *American Sociological Review* 1957, 22, 58–67.

77. Torrance, E. Paul. A theory of leadership and interpersonal behavior under stress. In *Leadership and Interpersonal Behavior,* Luigi Petrullo and Bernard M. Bass (eds.). New York: Holt, Rinehart & Winston, Inc., 1961.

78. White, Ralph and Lippitt, Ronald. Leader behavior and member reaction in three "social climates." In *Group Dynamics,* Dorwin Cartwright and Alvin Zander (eds.). Evanston, Ill.: Row, Peterson & Company, 1960.

79. Whyte, Wiliam F., Jr. *Street Corner Society.* Chicago: University of Chicago Press, 1955.

80. Wolman, Benjamin. Leadership and group dynamics. *The Journal of Social Psychology* 1956, 43, 11–25.

7

Supervision and Control

Supervision Styles

Supervision and control can be considered the exercise of formal, organizationally legitimate authority. The person playing the supervisory role is selected by his superiors for this role and consequently has their, and presumably the organization's, goals in mind, over and above individual and group goals. He may also exercise leadership, an informal amount of control or influence over subordinates occurring within the formal authority structure; thus, he may be "followed" without considering his formal authority position and its concomitant organizational rewards and punishments. "Supervisor" is, then, a generic term for industrial, business, and government executives and officials, military officers, superintendents, foremen and, in fact, anyone given formal authority by an organization over others.

As with "leadership, the three main styles of supervision are autocratic (authoritarian), democratic, and laissez-faire; the style that works best is the one most in agreement with the needs of the followers. Generally, however, it can be said that the democratic approach is the most satisfying to those being supervised and leads to the greatest productivity. Autocratic styles can be effective, as in the military, where a highly structured situation is needed to push men to the limits of performance. However, a laissez-faire approach to supervision is meaningless, because if a group can make the necessary organizational decisions and administer rewards and punishments, no authority figure (supervisor) is needed. But for certain bureaucratic purposes, such as having a "figurehead" to "rubber-stamp" group decisions, a true laissez-faire supervisor may exist.

Comrey, Pfiffner, and Beem (14, 15) studied U. S. forest supervisors and office managers of the California State Department of Employment in order to relate effectiveness to supervisory style. The measure of effectiveness for forest supervisors was "how well the forests were accomplishing their objectives," and for the office managers, their performance rating by area managers. For both groups, the authors found the supervisors of the more highly rated forests and offices to be "more democratic with their top assistants, allowing them greater participation in running the organization . . . more sympathetic . . . more willing and able to help top subordinates in their work" (15, p. 66). In studying researchers in a large government medical research organization, Pelz indicated "the level of individuals' scientific performance is found to be higher under . . . a [laboratory] chief who gives neither complete autonomy nor excessive direction, but who . . . gives them the opportunity to make their own decision" (63, p. 325). This, of course, implies that stronger motivations to reach scientific goals occur under the democratic supervisory approach.

An authoritarian approach seems to some to connote a lack of consideration for the employees, but Stanton (70) presents evidence to the contrary. He compared supervisors' attitudes toward supervision in two companies, one having authoritarian management and the other democratic. In the democratic company, the primary obligation was to the employees—allowing employee participation in policies and some flexibility of rules and procedures. For the authoritarian company, the obligation to the employees was secondary; employee participation was non-existent and rules were rigidly enforced. He found no significant difference between the attitudes of supervisors of both companies toward how much consideration should be shown employees. Thus, a company's management can be authoritarian and still be considerate of the feelings of its employees (p. 26). If actual interpersonal relations transcend formal approaches, then it is possible that authoritarian supervision per se does not actually lower productivity. Productivity may lean more heavily on employee consideration or a developed sense of loyalty. In studying two welfare agencies, Blau and Scott (6) found that productivity was not lowered under conditions of authoritarian supervision, because "supervisors who had won the loyal support of their subordinates were most successful in commanding willing compliance with their directives and in stimulating effort" (p. 163)* and their authoritarian style becomes of secondary importance in affecting productivity. Blau and Scott also suggest that "supervisors whose approach is inconsistent with their disposition ["normal mode of conduct"] . . . are apparently less likely to command the loyalty of subordinates" (p. 159)* as is true of supervisors who express primary loyalty to their superiors rather than to their workers. When the supervisor is establishing this loyalty he should be aware of the possible "danger that relations between supervisors and subordinates will be 'too good,' since the supervisor may become personally involved in the network of relations among subordinates to the extent of being confined by them" (6, p. 153)†. A supervisor can create social obligations or a quasi-loyalty of his workers for himself by not using all his authority at any one time. The greater the supervisor's "knowledge of formal requirements, group norms, and actual practice— the greater will be his ability to judge which operating rules can be ignored without impairing efficiency" (6, p. 143)‡.

Bowers has stated that some have noted "supervisory styles tend to be similar between adjoining hierarchical levels within an organization" (7, p. 135). He offers two possible explanations for this. Lower level supervisors imitate behavior of higher level supervisors because this is the path to rewards and success (p. 135). Another explanation would be that all supervisors tend to think alike, and hence behave similarly, because those who do the promoting promote those who think as they do. In studying 1000 foremen from 19 Midwestern plants, Balma, Maloney, and Lawshe found a low, but significant, "positive relationship between foreman identification-with-management scores and management ratings of how well the various foremen's work groups are doing their present job" (2, p. 373). In other words, foremen who were most like their supervisors were rated higher than other foremen. It would be expected the foremen with the higher identification scores with management would be more likely to be promoted, since they were also perceived as being more effective in their jobs. And, conversely, the authors suggest that a foreman's identification with management is related to aspirations of upward mobility—those with the strongest identifications have more education and are younger. Since "no relationship was found between employee attitude toward the foreman and his identification with man-

* From *Formal Organizations: A Comparative Study* by Peter M. Blau and W. Richard Scott, published by the Chandler Publishing Company, San Francisco. Copyright © 1962 by Chandler Publishing Company. Reprinted by permission.
  † *Ibid.*
  ‡ *Ibid.*

agement" (p. 377), no relationship could be surmised between employee attitudes toward supervision and work group productivity (p. 377). Of course, other studies have found relationships between other attitudes and productivity, but so far no significant relationship has been found between identification and productivity.

Differential Perception of Supervisors

All things considered, there is probably no one best way to supervise; as with leadership, the success of a particular style depends upon the personality of those who "follow." In any case, there seems to be little agreement as to what constitutes good supervision. In studying U. S. Air Force officers, noncommissioned officers (NCO's) and airmen, Moore and Smith showed that "what is considered a good NCO in the eyes of an officer is likely to be different from what is considered a good NCO from the standpoint of an airman or NCO" (56, p. 432). The indication is that ideas about supervision are partly a function of one's position in the organizational hierarchy. In a Midwestern cereal-processing plant, Besco and Lawshe found "no relationship between subordinate and superior perceptions of leadership behavior of the same foremen" (5, p. 579). They said there could be two reasons for this: Either the foremen's superiors or subordinates perceived the same behavior as being different or the foremen acted differently for their superiors than for their subordinates. It is also possible the superiors and subordinates were judging or rating the foremen on different dimensions. Meyer (54) administered a questionnaire about job responsibilities and functions to foremen and their supervisors, the general foremen, in a General Electric Company plant. The results indicated "a fairly high level of disagreement between foremen and general foremen regarding the responsibilities of the foreman" (p. 445). Both foremen rated "least effective" and those rated "most effective" agreed, theoretically, with general foremen on the required amount of job responsibility. However, in practice, foremen rated "most effective" by general foremen "characteristically claimed more responsibility for job functions than did 'least effective' foremen" (p. 446). Rosen (68) studied a plant manager, seven division, and thirty-seven section managers in an industrial plant. All of these personnel listed sixteen "occupational role prescriptions," defining certain job behaviors relating to supervision, in rank order of their perceived importance. Within each supervisory level, there was significant agreement as to the "proper" occupational role. However, "division management's prediction of their superior's demands were not significantly related to

What is considered a good supervisor by top management may not be the same as by line personnel

the actual demands . . . [but] predictions with regard to subordinate demands . . . related to the actual demands" (p. 32). The section managers did, though, accurately predict the division manager's demands (p. 32). The plant manager could not accurately predict his subordinate's role prescriptions. As Rosen suggests, there does appear to be a communication problem.

Even where a manager previously held his subordinate's job, there is not necessarily any better communication. Maier, Hoffman, and Read (49) studied 20 superior-subordinate pairs of supervisors where the superior once held the subordinate's job and 20 where the superior had not. "Managers who had held their subordinate's jobs were in no better communication with their subordinates than were managers who had not held their subordinate's jobs" (p. 8). Their explanation was that subordinates whose superiors once held their job were more ambitious to be promoted than the other subordinates, and so were "less communicative than the less ambitious ones" (p. 9). Differential perceptions between supervisory levels about the proper role to play in supervision are due, not only to individual preferences and ineffective communication between levels, but also to considerations of empathy. If empathy is defined as understanding another's attitudes and feelings, then it would be expected that supervisors with empathy for higher or lower hierarchical levels would have more similar perceptions of supervisory role prescriptions.

Browne and Shore have hypothesized: "the individual who will be most successful in influencing the actions of a group . . . will be the individual who knows the thinking of the group best" (9, p. 112). They used 83 men at four different hierarchical levels in a metal tubing manufacturing company. Each was given a questionnaire and was asked to predict the attitudes of the other men on economic and social issues and on job satisfaction. The higher level personnel were found to predict the attitudes of the lower level better than the lower level predicted higher level attitudes. Since the higher levels must manage the lower levels, it is not too surprising that they do know the attitudes of those they manage. In other words, being an effective supervisor implies empathy with subordinates, while being an effective worker does not. This problem of industrial conflict, then, may arise "more as the result of lack of understanding of management personnel by nonsupervisory personnel" (9, p. 115) than vice versa. Foa (25) asked 361 Israeli factory workers and their 51 foremen to predict each other's responses. His findings indicate that when a worker "is oriented toward his peer group he is somewhat less likely to succeed in empathizing the foreman" (p. 7), but when "the foreman is oriented toward the workers, the worker is more successful in empathizing him" (pp. 7–8). However, when a worker actually perceives the foreman to be worker-oriented, he will not be successful in empathizing the foreman because of his familiarity with the foreman's attitude and behavior cues. This fixedness of perception naturally clouds his observation of the actual cues.

Nagle (57) found for supervisors of the office department of a large industrial company that the more favorable the workers' attitude toward the supervisor, the more favorable their attitude toward the company, indicating a halo effect. If the supervisor were sensitive to the attitudes of his subordinates, chances are the employees' attitudes toward the supervisor would be favorable (p. 227). Although the author disclaims any cause-effect relationship, he does report that the more sensitive or empathetic the foreman is toward his subordinates, the higher the productivity of that group. Patton found, to the contrary, in the textile industry that "empathetic ability was no greater among supervisors who were considered by management to be the best than those considered by management to be the worst" (62, p. 285). The disagreement between these two findings can best be explained by an intervening variable, that of favorable attitudes toward the supervisor. Nagle (57) found favorable attitudes toward supervision usually go with high productivity, as others (42, 47) have found. When this condition exists, empathy of the superior for the subordinate relates mostly to the productivity factor; when empathy does not exist, its absence has no effect upon productivity. Turner (76) in conducting a study in an automobile assembly plant, found a greater degree of positive sentiment or feeling between worker and foreman when interaction between them was frequent and included "informal, friendly contacts in addition to those required in the course of the work" (p. 16). Such positive sentiment will be at its strongest when both the foreman and worker initiate interaction at about the same frequency (p. 16). *Communication,* then, can smooth interpersonal relations and attitudes and increase empathy. In spite of "effective" communication, all attitudes cannot be positive and empathy cannot be complete, simply because of personality differences. Differential perceptions between and within worker and supervisory levels will always exist.

Differential Self-conceptions and Behavior

As the occupants of different hierarchical levels view those at other levels from their peculiar perspective, so also are their self-perceptions commensurate with their level—that is, there is a tendency to conceive of oneself in ways appropriate to the hierarchical level occupied. Management, as opposed to non-management personnel, "perceive of themselves in terms of leadership qualities . . . they see themselves . . . as relatively dominant types of individuals . . . as possessing a good degree of initiative and independence of thought and action" (65, p. 106). Coates and Pellegrin (13) report similar findings for 50 executives in the South compared with supervisors felt they had more initiative and energy. In Porter's study of 320 line workers and 463 management personnel the line workers presented more of a follower image (65, p. 107). As Ghiselli has stated, "persons at different occupational levels perceive themselves in different ways" (30, p. 175). Each level has its own group norms, and deviation from them can lead to censure from not only peers but also the other levels. Someone in a lower level position "who to his superior behaves like . . . a person in a higher occupation would be expected to be less favorably regarded by his superior" (30, p. 174). Differential perceptions and their correlate, differential behaviors, are to some degree forced on each level by the others.

The basic follower role of the lower levels (65) has been characterized by Merenda and Clarke (52): "Members of the upper occupational class appear to be more aggressive and socially confident while those of the lower stratum appear to be more placid and submissive" (p. 291). In studying 208 executives and 143 supervisors of a large grocery chain, Guilford (35) found the executives as a group were more "(1) sociable, (2) free from depression, (3) emotionally stable, (4) happy-go-lucky, (5) active, (6) ascendant or socially bold, (7) self-confident, (8) calm and composed, (9) objective, (10) agreeable, and (11) cooperative" (p. 232) than were the supervisors. Cause and effect statements are as difficult to make here as they were about leadership traits; probably, however, these traits are due largely to the effect of freedom and job security that exists for the executive. The like can be said of social dominance, or extroversion. Meyer and Pressel (53) administered a psychological test to five levels of a work hierarchy ranging from top executives to factory workers and clerks. They found a "trend for higher social dominance trait scores as the hierarchy ascends" (p. 78) from workers to executives. These scores were independent of age and education variables.

Executives need to be more extroverted than workers because they interact more with people and must deal, to some extent, with personnel management. At this level, extroversion can flourish and be rewarded; hence, the opportunity "causes" the exercise. These researchers found a "trend . . . for better [personality] adjustment scores as the hierarchy ascends" (p. 78)—probably an effect, more than a cause, of being at a higher level.

Coates and Pellegrin present evidence, based on Southern executives and supervisors, that "supervisors tended to be acutely aware of the handicaps of their socio-cultural backgrounds, education and training and occupational opportunities" (13, p. 219). Both supervisors and execu-

Greater job security can make the executive more effective and easier to get along with

tives were aware of the rewards and penalties associated with their positions. These differential self-conceptions can, as Dalton (16) has indicated, be partly responsible for staff-line conflicts. Dalton's study in three industrial plants revealed that line and staff personnel belonged to different social status groups (16, p. 347) accounting for different perceptions of their jobs and opportunities. Staff men were younger with more education than line managers and consequently had stronger promotional desires and a different outlook on their work. In welfare agencies, Blau and Scott (6) found conflicts between line (the social caseworkers) and staff (the accounting section) over the amount of money to be given to those on welfare. "Such conflicts are not motivated by self-interests; rather they result from each party's devotion to its job" (6, p. 174)*. Since each group's self-conceptions are different, each person's approach to the task will be somewhat different and staff-line conflict could result.

Based on 320 male Air Force personnel, ranging from corporals to lieutenant colonels, Hetzler reports that "lower status [rank] leaders favored somewhat more directive leadership techniques" (41, p. 703) than higher ranked leaders. Differing amounts of self-confidence among the personnel at the different levels seems to account for this finding. Kipnis and Lane report "findings that junior Petty Officers exercised less direct leadership and placed more reliance upon unofficial referrals to superiors or upon placing a subordinate on report" (45, p. 294). Note that *directive* leadership means autocratic in style while *direct* leadership means actual leadership rather than supervision. Having less self-confidence, lower-level personnel tend to be more autocratic and strict, not wanting to get into a situation where their authority may be challenged. Hetzler also indicates "leaders of greater advancement potential and present attainment look primarily to their peers and superiors for both status gratification and further reward" (41, p. 705), while lower level "leaders" looked to their subordinates. One explanation might be that upper level personnel receive their power and authority primarily from their superiors while lower level personnel receive it primarily from their followers—hence their orientations.

The various levels of management and lower-level personnel have different perceptions of themselves and of other levels. However, Ghiselli suggests "the usual classification of persons as management versus line-personnel may not be wholly adequate" (31, p. 543). His conclusions are based on a sample of 113 top management people (president, vice president, head of major operations), 176 middle managers (division or department heads, staff specialists), 172 lower managers (who put into

* From *Formal Organizations: A Comparative Study* by Peter M. Blau and W. Richard Scott, published by the Chandler Publishing Company, San Francisco. Copyright © 1962 by Chandler Publishing Company. Reprinted by permission.

effect middle-management directives), and 319 line workers—all in many different companies throughout the country. Based on intelligence, supervisory ability, initiative, and self-assurance scores, the top and middle management people as a group scored higher than did lower management and line workers as a group. This seems to indicate that the simple black-white division between management and line workers does not invariably hold.

Supervisory Dimensions and Relevant
Attitudes Surrounding Them

The question arises, "What do supervisors do?" Guest (34) has done a minute-by-minute analysis of 56 production foremen in an automobile assembly plant. While the specific behavior of these foremen is not necessarily typical of other foremen in other jobs, it does give some indication of the behavior present in one segment of industry. Guest (34, p. 481) found that about 92% of the foremen's activity could be accounted for by nine behavior categories. These categories and the percentage of time spent in them are: quality (18.2%), work progress (13.2%), personnel administration and relations (21.4%), performing the operation (8.1%), working with tools, jigs, fixtures (8.1%), materials (8.0%), employee job performance (7.6%), production schedule (5.2%), and grievances (2.0%). The poorer foremen seemed to spend more time in actually performing some of the operations rather than "supervising" them. In terms of personal contact with others, these foremen spent 26.4% of their time with subordinates, 7.0% with peers (the other foremen), 5.7% with superiors, and 7.8% with the service personnel (p. 482). Prien (66), after studying 30 supervisors comes up with seven factors describing what supervisors do: (1) manufacturing process supervision, day-to-day emergency procedures; (2) manufacturing process administration, day-to-day routine operations; (3) employee supervision, "face-to-face relationships of a personal nature"; (4) manpower coordination and administration, making effective use of workers; (5) employee contact and communications; (6) work organization, planning, and preparation; and (7) union-management relations. Kunnath and Kerr (46) studied the behavior of 32 boards of directors of companies ranging in size from 50 to 25,000 employees. As a rule, "the topics given most frequent attention by boards are those related to immediate corporate survival, while those less frequently treated topics tend to be related . . . to the internal workings of the company" (p. 67). The most frequent topics discussed were "future business prospects, competition, quantity of output, distribution, and the business cycle" (p. 66). Their behavior, then, was oriented toward these goals, implying a more general, sweeping approach to long-term problems.

Case study approaches like these have their limitations, because the behavior elicited is not only a function of the complex interactions among supervisor, subordinates, and superiors, but also can be explained in different words even when its import is the same. In short, there is no standardization of categories to provide universality. A factor analysis approach is somewhat better in this regard; but as previously mentioned, different words can still be used for the same behavior categories. The main advantage of factor analysis is that, if the same questionnaires are used in each study and the same supervisory dimensions are present, then the same *factors* (rather than exact wording) will appear. In other words, the factor approach can lead to standardization much better than can an analysis of case studies. For instance, Stogdill, *et al.* (71), in studying 470 naval officers of all ranks in 12 types of Naval organizations (submarines, destroyers, command staffs, air stations, etc.), found by factor analysis that "groups of persons in similar specialties in different kinds of organizations will exhibit similar patterns of performance" (p. 177). (This means attending meetings, conferring with assistants, writing reports, planning, delegating duties, etc.). The next step is to see if persons in different specialties supervise in the same dimensions.

Research results do indicate, however, that there is no one set of factors that describes supervisory dimensions for all types of organizations. Studies have taken the form of questionnaires given to supervisors to determine the "main" supervisory duties. Stogdill, Goode, and Day (71) gave questionnaires to 55 corporate presidents' immediate staff to answer questions about the presidents' behavior. Emerging from the analysis were 10 factors, indicative of these executives' behavior: (1) production emphasis; (2) role enactment, performing leadership functions; (3) orientation toward supervisors, i.e. "comfortable associations with persons in positions of high status"; (4) consideration of employees; (5) tolerance of uncertainty and delay; (6) representation of member interests, acting on behalf of the group; (7) tolerance of member freedom of action, allowing subordinates some freedom of initiative; (8) persuasiveness; (9) reconciliation of conflicting demands, dealing with disorder and conflict; (10) predictive accuracy, predicting future outcomes of events. If one assumes that the supervisory behavior of corporate presidents is "good" or they would not retain their jobs, then he can conclude that the potential supervisor should score high on these dimensions.

Peres (64) states that such factors "can serve as a basis for evaluating the performance of supervisors" (p. 410). He had 372 supervisors at the Sandia Corporation describe the best supervisors they knew at Sandia. The six factors that best describe good supervisory behavior are: (1)

establishment of work climate, maintaining definite performance standards; (2) management ethics, "above board in his management dealings"; (3) self and subordinate development by off- and on-the-job training; (4) maturity and sensitivity; (5) knowledge and execution of corporate policies and procedures; and (6) technical job knowledge.

Roach (67) based his factor analysis on the managers of 245 white collar supervisors. His factors were: (1) personal compliance, "does what is expected of him"; (2) job knowledge; (3) direction of group performance, planning and organizing; (4) rewarding performance of his subordinates; (5) company loyalty; (6) acceptance of responsibility; (7) maintaining group spirit (morale); (8) personal drive (motivation); (9) impartiality in dealing with subordinates; (10) poise and bearing (self-confidence); (11) consideration of workers. These three factor studies point up the disagreements about supervision between companies (the intra-company disagreement has already been mentioned)—what is important to one company is not necessarily important to another. One factor that explicitly appears in two of the studies (71, 67), consideration of the employees by the supervisor, appears implicitly in maturity and sensitivity factor of Peres (64). This factor probably accounts for a good proportion of the favorable attitudes of workers toward their supervisors; that is, when consideration is high, all other things being equal, favorable attitudes will tend to be present.

Turner (75) studied 202 automobile assembly line workers who had been on the job about twelve years. Only 44% of them said they "got along 'very well or fairly well' " with the foreman. They disliked the mechanical pacing and repetitiveness of the job and felt, consequently, they were badly treated by the company. In short, there was little consideration present, and their attitudes were negative. However, "because an assembly-line foreman exercises little control over the nature of the worker's immediate job, the workers' attitudes toward the job and the foreman are independent of each other" (75, p. 110). At Swift and Company, Obrochta (59) compared the attitudes of workers and foremen about the company, job, each other, and the union. Foremen had more favorable attitudes toward the company than did the workers, probably because the company was more considerate of their needs than of the workers' needs, that is, the foremen felt more involved because they were higher in the hierarchy. Agreement on attitudes toward the job was at the 69% level, toward the union 78%, and toward the plant's union leadership only 54.6%. Again, the level of the hierarchy one occupies conditions his attitudes. The workers regarded the foremen more favorably than the foremen did them, perhaps because the workers felt that favorable attitudes toward their immediate superiors might lead to rewards, or even to more consideration on the foremen's part. Identification (perceiving oneself as having similar attitudes and opinions) either with management or with the rank-and-file can affect foremen's attitudes as well. Halpern (37) found that for all foremen who identify with the rank-and-file worker, "foremen in unionized firms are somewhat more likely to say that success is the result of external forces ["luck, business conditions, and 'who you know' "] than are foremen in nonunion firms" (p. 85). Furthermore, of those identifying with the workers, 79% of foremen in nonunion plants were satisfied with their jobs versus 47% of the foremen in unionized plants. In union plants where seniority is of prime importance, external factors are perceived to count more in success than internal factors such as skill. Consequently, job satisfaction is lower. If, however, foremen identify with management, there is little difference in the attitudes of union versus nonunion foremen. In this case they have developed management's way of looking at the organization and look upon success accordingly.

Consideration and Structuring Factors

Consideration has been mentioned throughout this chapter as being important to supervision. A standardized test called the Leadership Opinion Questionnaire can be used to obtain an accurate measure of something called "consideration and structuring" (initiating structure). Here consideration is defined as concern for subordinates' feelings—"behavior indicative of friendship, mutual trust and respect, and good 'human relations' " (38). For the supervisor, structuring "defines the role he expects each member to assume" (22). Fleishman and Harris report that these two factors are basically independent of each other and measure separate supervisory dimensions (22). They have been considered important dimensions of effective supervision by many researchers.

Bass (3) found for 53 lower-level supervisors of a petrochemical refinery a significant relationship "between the extent to which a supervisor believed he ought to be considerate of his subordinates and the extent to which he was rated a successful supervisor by his superiors two years later" (p. 346). In another study, Bass (4) studied 42 sales supervisors in a food products company and found "supervisors with favorable attitudes toward being considerate . . . were rated significantly more effective approximately 3 years later" (p. 517); in both, the structuring measure was not significantly related to the effective criterion.

Note that there may be a difference between having favorable attitudes toward being considerate and *actually* being so. Halpin (38) points out this difference in his study of B-29 and B-50 aircraft commanders. These commanders realize the value of possessing consideration and structuring factors, but "the evidence suggests that on the whole the aircraft commander's knowledge of how he should behave as a leader has little bearing upon how he is perceived as behaving by the members of his crew" (p. 84).

For other B-29 crews, possession of consideration and "initiation of structure behavior is also related to a more rapid development of friendship and confidence" (11, p. 87) within the crews. Based on 80 work groups in a wholesale pharmaceutical company, Parker (60) found "supervisory consideration was correlated with favorable attitudes toward supervision but appeared unrelated to group performance . . . . initiating structure was weakly related to favorable attitudes toward supervision" (p. 326) but not to performance. He found group productivity would be high when workers related job performance with job security. Lawshe and Nagle (47) did find that for office workers a more favorable attitude toward one's superior was related to higher productivity. In a study done in the Overhaul and Repair Department of the Naval Air Station in San Diego involving over 1,000 workers, Wilson, Beem, and Comrey indicate that "supervisors in both the 'high' and 'low' [productivity] shops were described by their . . . subordinates as (1) more helpful, (2) more sympathetic, (3) less hypercritical" (78, p. 314). In this case, both high and low productivity were associated with favorable attitudes toward supervision. As Chapter 2 has pointed out, however, favorable attitudes will lead to greater productivity in a direct way only when the greater productivity satisfies a need of the individual worker.   Practically, it could be a need to respond favorably by higher output to the supervisory style. Attitudes toward supervision do correlate directly with grievances, though. "Departments with high worker grievance rates contained foremen who perceived their own supervisors as expecting them to lead with a lower degree of consideration and a higher degree of structuring" (21, p. 158). For 57 production foremen in a motor truck manufacturing plant, Fleishman and Harris report "in general, low consideration and high structure go with high grievances and turnover (22, p. 52). They point out that consideration is the stronger factor, as "both grievances and turnover were highest in groups having low consideration foremen regardless of the degree of structuring behavior shown by those same foremen" (p. 53). Perhaps, with low consideration, high structuring appears threatening but with high consideration, high structuring appears supportive (p. 54). As with the other relationships studied, the cause-effect inferences are not clearcut; as these authors indicate, high grievances may cause workers to view their foremen as being inconsiderate, but initiating too much structure may in turn cause grievances and turnover.

In another study of Fleishman's, "the higher people were in the plant hierarchy, the less consideration they felt the workers should get and the more structuring they felt should be initiated" (21, p. 158). However, another study by Fleishman indicated higher managers favored less structuring (23). Oaklander and Fleishman (58) studied 118 supervisors in three New York hospitals to see if stress was related to consideration and structuring. They measured stress on both an intraunit basis (cooperativeness of employees) and an interunit basis (between supervisors). "Higher consideration was significantly related to lower intraunit stress" (p. 527), but no relation was found to interunit stress; there is no guarantee that a supervisor's consideration for subordinates, his own and others, implies consideration for other supervisors. For two of the three hospitals, "department heads scoring higher on structure tended to have significantly lower interdepartmental stress" (p. 527), but the relationship of structuring to intraunit stress was not significant. With similar operating structures, standardization of procedures is possible thereby reducing interdepartmental stress caused by conflicting procedures.

Supervisory Orientation

Two other important dimensions of supervision relate to the orientation of the supervisor with respect to how "close" he supervises, and whether or not he is "human-relations" minded. Both of these affect or are affected by worker productivity. A 1950 study by Katz, Maccoby, and Morse (44) in part of the Prudential Insurance Company sought to find the relationship between supervisory practices and productivity. They report "the section heads of the low producing sections supervise their employees more closely than do the section heads of the high producing groups" (p. 17). The section heads of the high producing groups were also more human-relations oriented, meaning they were employee oriented, than were the low production supervisors who were production or technically oriented. Similar results were reported by Kahn and Katz (43) based on other studies of railroad and tractor factory workers. They attribute this orientation in large part to "the organizational climate which exists at higher levels in the management hierarchy" (43, p. 560). Ghiselli and Barthol (32) obtained profiles of 267 "good" and "bad" supervisors as judged by their superiors. The good supervisor "views his responsibilities broadly . . . feels he must exercise certain independence of thought and action . . . orientation toward production is through people" (p. 243). On the other hand, the poor supervisor "seems to have a narrow approach to his job . . . does not show any need to understand and respect others" (p. 243).

Patchen feels that "where supervision is close, employees might be expected to leave the responsibility for good work to the foreman (61, p. 279). His study was done in a plastic materials manufacturing company where questionnaires were given to 17 different work groups to determine why there are differences in group performance norms. For his sample, the highest production came from groups "whose foremen go to bat for their men and encourage efficiency" (p. 283). Either encouraging efficiency, or going to bat, alone was not sufficient to obtain high producing work groups. Foremen who go to bat for workers but do not encourage production may give the impression that efficiency is not important; on the other hand, a call to more production may be resented if the foreman does not stand up for his men (p. 284). Patchen defines close supervision as "frequent *checking* on subordinates' work, and *not* reducing subordinates' freedom to do the work in their own way" (p. 290). Hence, encouraging efficiency, in part by frequent checking, does serve to increase productivity if the foreman also adequately represents his men. (Of course, frequent checking does not necessarily mean close supervision as defined by other researchers.)

When a supervisor links rewards and punishments with production, he can directly influence production. Argyle, Gardner, and Cioffi report for 90 foremen in eight British manufacturing factories that "foremen of high-producing sections exercised general rather than close supervision and were relatively more democratic and non-punitive than foremen of low-producing sections" (1, p. 35). They suggest if punitive supervision creates aggression, then "low output could be regarded as a form of aggression against the company and the foreman" (p. 36). Day and Hamblin (19) found for college women performing an assembly task in a laboratory with the experimenter playing the role of supervisor that "close supervision produced a significant and large increment in aggressive feelings toward the supervisor" (pp. 505–507). Close supervision did not affect job satisfaction nor evoke verbal aggression toward co-workers, but it did reduce productivity (p. 507). Punitive supervision (involving overt punishment) "resulted in a large, significant increase in verbal aggression toward the supervisor" (p. 507) and also reduced productivity.

Fiedler's ASo (Assumed Similarity between opposites) criterion was used on 41 supervisors in the San Antonio, Texas, Post Office by Carp, Vitola, and McLanathan (10). They found supervisors who were somewhat socially distant from their subordinates had the more productive workers. This finding is in agreement with those presented in Chapter 6; namely, the most effective leaders were the more socially distant from their group. Specifically, "effective supervisors stay psychologically close enough to maintain contact with group members and far enough to deal objectively with poor performance" (10, p. 80). Concurrent with this, supervisors with a high knowledge of human relations skills, as measured by a test, had the best producing work groups. Marcus (50), in studying a welfare organization, finds that attitudes toward supervision create splinter groups of high cohesiveness, since the workers consult more with their peers than with supervisors; eventually part of the supervisory function is destroyed. In summary: "supervisors who are perceived as adhering to rules are not liked as much as the more permissive ones and the former have groups with lower production rates" (p. 19)—all of this in agreement with other research cited.

Is it possible that work group habits could cause a style of supervision to be elicited? High output may cause a supervisor not to be production oriented; however, it is more likely that the relationship is vice versa—that supervision affects output more than output affects supervision. Argyle, Gardner, and Cioffi (1) suggest that an external factor could affect both output and supervision. For instance, jobs with high turnover rates cause output to be relatively low and supervision relatively close. They suggest supervision will have its greatest effect when work output is not dependent on machine pacing and when a wage incentive system is not in force. With the latter, motivation is controlled primarily by the desire to earn more money rather than by the supervisor's persuasive or permissive techniques.

In summary, there are "many research findings showing that some variables representative of 'good' human relations practice are in fact positively and significantly related to performance" (42, p. 357). Performance changes of the order of 7 to 15% can usually be expected (1, p. 24). Indik, Georgopoulos, and Seashore state that the human-relations oriented or "supportive supervisor, by providing a secure environment, reduces the amount of energy diverted by subordinates from production to self-protective and ego-sustaining activities (42, p. 360). They feel performance levels will be high under conditions of effective communication between supervisor and subordinates, satisfaction with supervisory behavior, empathy in both directions, and work autonomy (p. 371). In other words, "the kinds of supervisory behavior which are appropriate and are responded to favorably by subordinates vary not only with the past experiences and values of the subordinates but also vary with the traditions of the working situation" (48, p. 324). The implication is that there is no right or wrong way to supervise, for supervision is "always an adaptive process. . . . A leader to be effective, must always adapt his behavior to fit the expectations, values and interpersonal skills" (48, p. 327) of his subordinates.

Aspects of Executive Behavior

Any mystery about executives and their behavior "is probably generated mainly by a misguided desire to eliminate the complications in favor of some simple common denominator of executive virtue" (8, p. 550). Leadership and supervision traits by themselves only show part of the picture. A general profile of executives by Braybrooke (8) does give some resources, beyond mere traits, that contribute to effective supervision. He defines two main types: "relatively transferable resources" and "relatively nontransferable resources." The former category includes "energy and application (appetite for work) . . . an air and style of leadership . . . skill in bargaining . . . universal connections" (pp. 544–545), or acquaintances in many walks of life. These resources are company-independent—an executive always has them available because they are parts of himself. Nontransferable resources involve "a manner appropriate to the trade . . . local connections . . . judgment of men" (pp. 545–546) based on specific experience with men around him. Applications of this can be seen in many studies, such as the one by Dalton (18) involving a case study of three factories and one department store in the central United States.

If an organization is perfect, says Braybrooke, "would not every specialized power be delegated to some specialized functionary? The man at the top would be left with nothing . . . to do" (8, p. 534). Executives result, then, from the existence of imperfect organizations. By this reasoning, it is their task to delegate duties. Zaleznik (79) would argue that executives have three other functions: homeostatic, mediative, and proactive. The homeostatic function assures "the internal stability of the organization from internal press" while the mediative one creates internal change to cope with external pressures. The proactive function "induces change in the environment to conform to the creative use of resources available within the organization" (p. 158). The executive task is to coordinate these functions and optimally mix them, playing one against the other.

Henry (40) has suggested that a fear of failure may motivate executives to do well in their vocation. Executives have a need to be active and aggressive and to develop and use the resources of the sort that Braybrooke has mentioned. Miner and Culver (55) studied 44 executive officers of large corporations in the East; they presented them with several sets of pictures which they were to arrange into a meaningful sequence and write a short story about. "What is characteristic of the executives is the specification of a particular kind of anxiety, namely, that which has illness or injury as its object" (p. 350). This is another way of saying the executive has a fear of failure as "illness would deprive him of the capacity to satisfy his need for activity" (p. 352). Compared to a control group of college professors of the same age, the executives tended to rely more on others for help in solving their problems. The executive "is projecting his own quite real feelings of helplessness in dealing with complex job demands" (55, p. 352). Such feelings often lead to the selection of an "assistant-to" who will function as a staff aide and help in the problem-solving, decision-making area. Whisler (77) has done a study with four kinds of "assistant-to" personnel: the "assistant to the president" in business organizations, "aide-de-camp" in the military, "executive assistant" in the federal government, and the "assistant to the city manager." He finds "a greater percentage of those organizations that regularly rotate top managers will use the assistant-to, than those that do not" (p. 208). Incoming managers in these organizations will need information immediately and the assistant-to can supply it. The assistant-to will be needed less frequently "in those organizations experiencing rapid change in size, scope of activities, and technological characteristics than in more stable organizations" (p. 208). Under these conditions the organizational information changes too fast for any assistant-to to handle; the executive can gain the information just as fast himself. When the executive experiences interpersonal relations problems, he will often request an assistant-to to act as a buffer.

Success for the assistant-to was closely related to the agreement his social and educational background had with that of his immediate boss (77, p. 211). This finding was the subject of a study done by Dalton (17) with 226 managers ranging from foremen to staff heads in a large organization. He compared their positions within the company with certain "informal" factors, such as education, club memberships and other social activities, ethnic background, and religious and political affiliations. His findings indicate that advancement was due more to having the "right" informal factors than to the ability to advance plant goals. Coates and Pellegrin (12) did a replication of this study with 50 executives and 50 first line supervisors in a Southern metropolitan area. The *less* important informal career factors (as opposed to the important formal career factors of intelligence, ability, honesty, etc.) were, contrary to Dalton's findings, religious and political affiliations, ethnic background, and membership in fraternal orders. The more important informal factors that related to success were membership in professional, civic, and social organizations, family social connections, recreational activities (and whom done with), judicious consumption as opposed to conspicuous consumption, the influence of the wife on other executives' wives, maintaining and establishing friendship at all levels, and "acquisition of the attitudes, values, and behavior patterns of successful superiors." It is not surprising that personality and social factors are important, since executives must work closely with those around them. Ghiselli presents evidence that "men who perceive themselves in about the same way as the average person of their age [are] most likely to be successful" (30, p. 46). Those who promote others like to promote those who have similar perceptions.

Trait approaches to predict executive success are, of course, common. Consideration was a trait that seemed to permeate all supervisory levels.

A trait that seems to relate just to executive or high-level supervision is nonconformity. An experiment carried out by Fleishman and Peters in a division of a soap and detergent manufacturer indicated that "managers who scored higher on 'conformity' ["do what is accepted and proper"] . . . were independently rated as less 'effective' by top management" (23, p. 141). For 63 civil servants in the Italian government, "individuals who are seen as manifesting patterns of traits that are idiosyncratic tend to be regarded as superior administrators" (28, p. 9). It is evident that being too creative or being too much of a nonconformist at lower supervisory levels can hamper success, while with the possession of authority, more idiosyncracies are tolerated, and even expected. General Patton carried two pearl-handled pistols on his side, but could he get by with it as a private? Ghiselli (28) suggests that the individuality possessed by executives may not directly relate to success but may cause or relate to other traits (initiative, for example) that *are* directly related to success.

Based on a review of the available literature, Goodacre (33) reports that successful managers have often been influenced in the past by other successful ones who as a composite "(a) set high clear standards, (b) delegate extensively, (c) inform people as to how they are performing, (d) assist when needed, (e) reward for performance" (pp. 133–134). General support of this composite has been presented by Gaudet and Carli (27) who sent questionnaires to 177 company presidents and vice presidents throughout the country. They asked them to consider two men they had promoted at the executive level, one of whom succeeded, one of whom failed, and to tell why. "Personality factors are found to be twice as important as 'knowledge lacks' as causes of executive failure" (p. 17). The failures on the knowledge side were lack of a breadth of knowledge and a lack in organization and administration knowledge. The main causes of failure, the "personality" side, were inabilities to "delegate responsibility . . . to analyze and evaluate . . . to judge people" (p. 17). Possession of these factors, then, leads to success in Goodacre's terms.

Span of Control

Span of control means the number of subordinates directly under the control of or reporting to an executive or supervisor. The notion of a limited span of control was first developed in the military and later adopted by other organizations. The basic theory was that there should be a specific, fixed number of subordinates under one supervisor. Deciding just how many there should be in a span presents the same difficulties as trying to determine optimal group size. Studies on the span of control in companies have been reported by Suojanen (73), Healey (39), and

Entwisle and Walton (20). Suojanen reports that 100 large companies have a median number of between 8 and 9 executives reporting to the president. Based on 260 industrial plants in Ohio, Healey found most of the top executives had a span of control of 8 or less. Entwisle and Walton report a median span of 5 people reporting to the presidents of 20 colleges and universities and also a span of 5 reporting to the heads of 14 small companies. There is evidence that as the size of the organization increases, the span of control increases to pass on more information. Healey says "the larger the unit, the higher the chief executive's span" (39, p. 116). Entwisle and Walton report a small positive correlation between size of company and size of span and a larger correlation between the two sizes for colleges and universities (20, p. 525).

Advocates of a particular span of control in the past have supported their claims by arithmetic arguments. They argue that the span of attention for a person extends to about 7 other people; therefore more than 7 in the span is not practicable. But as Entwisle and Walton (20) state, this attention span of 7 relates to simultaneous attention, and it is not likely that an executive will have to deal simultaneously with 7 subordinates. Others compute the number of interpersonal relationships possible by the formula $N(N - 1)/2$, where N equals the number of people. Thus, with 8 people (1 executive and 7 subordinates) there would be 28 relationships with every person interacting with every other person. This sounds like too many, but they cannot all happen at once—and some do not have to occur at all.

Gaiennie calls organization control "an attempt to measure degrees of conformity between the job organizational requirements, and the abilities and performance of job incumbents" (26, p. 290). Setting up a span of control is an attempt to meet this goal of matching personnel with organizational goals. Entwisle and Walton point out that the larger the span "the more possibilities there are for forming subgroups" (20, p. 530) that can threaten organizational leadership. On the other hand, Healey (39) reports the executives he studied wanted to keep their span low to avoid detail and exercise closer and "better" supervision. However, as has been pointed out, close supervision can help to lower personnel effectiveness, implying that a larger span of control is to be preferred.

Actually, the span of control is a function of "the training of the subordinates; the objectives of the group; the situation in which they find themselves; the communication facilities available to them" (36, p. 294). Often, an executive's span of control includes not just the formally designated subordinates but also so called "lower participants," such as secretaries, who find themselves in special situations with a direct communication link with higher-ranking personnel. These lower participants, as Mechanic (51) calls them, have considerably more power and influence than their organizational position would dictate. The longer a person is in an organization, the more access he has to information, people, and materials, and this gives him power over others who need the information, material, or access to others. "A person difficult to replace will have greater power than a person easily replaceable" (51, p. 358). If a low-ranking member "has important expert knowledge not available to high-ranking participants, he is likely to have power over them" (p. 357). Furthermore, when higher-ranking personnel do not devote much time and effort to a task, it is likely that lower-ranking personnel will obtain power relevant to it (p. 360). This situation can, of course, produce a span larger than is readily apparent to others.

Haire states the "idea of the span of control . . . is often discussed as if there were some absolute answer to the question—How many subordinates can a superior manage?—as if the span were a kind of inflexible constant in social organizations" (36, p. 294). It is not inflexible and depends on the organization and group that uses it. Because of the very nature of the behavioral sciences at present, attempts to list *optimal* courses of action usually have very little to recommend them.

Supervision and Control References

1. Argyle, Michael; Gardner, Godfrey and Cioffi, Frank. Supervisory methods related to productivity and absenteeism, and labour turnover. *Human Relations* 1958, 11, 23–40.

2. Balma, M. J.; Maloney, J. C. and Lawshe, C. H. The role of the foreman in modern industry: II, Foreman identification with management, work group productivity, and employee attitude toward the foreman. *Personnel Psychology* 1958, 11, 367–378.

3. Bass, Bernard M. Leadership opinions as forecasts of supervisory success. *Journal of Applied Psychology* 1956, 40, 345–346.

4. ———. Leadership opinions as forecasts of supervisory success: a replication. *Personnel Psychology* 1958, 11, 515–518.

5. Besco, Robert O. and Lawshe, C. H. Foreman leadership as perceived by superiors and subordinates. *Personnel Psychology* 1959, 12, 573–582.

6. Blau, Peter M. and Scott, W. Richard. *Formal Organizations*. San Francisco: Chandler Publishing Company, 1962.

7. Bowers, David G. Self-esteem and the diffusion of leadership style. *Journal of Applied Psychology,* 1963, 47, 135–140.

8. Braybrooke, David. The mystery of executive success re-examined. *Administrative Science Quarterly* 1964, 8, 533–560.

9. Browne, C. G. and Shore, Richard P. Leadership and predictive abstracting. *Journal of Applied Psychology* 1956, 40, 112–116.

10. Carp, Francis M.; Vitola, Bart M. and McLanathan, Frank L. Human relations knowledge and social distance set in supervisors. *Journal of Applied Psychology* 1963, 47, 78–80.

11. Christner, Charlotte A. and Hemphill, John K. Leader behavior of B-29 commanders and changes in crew members' attitudes toward the crew. *Sociometry* 1955, 18, 82–87.

12. Coates, Charles H. and Pellegrin, Roland J. Executives and supervisors: informal factors in differential bureaucratic promotion. *Administrative Science Quarterly* 1957, 2, 200–215.

13. ————. Executives and supervisors: contrasting self-conceptions of each other. *American Sociological Review* 1957, 22, 217–220.

14. Comrey, A. L.; Pfiffner, J. M. and Beem, Helen P. Factors influencing organizational effectiveness. I. The U. S. Forest Survey. *Personnel Psychology* 1952, 5, 307–328.

15. ————. Factors influencing organizational effectiveness II. The department of employment survey. *Personnel Psychology* 1953, 6, 65–79.

16. Dalton, Melville. Conflicts between staff and line managerial officers. *American Sociological Review* 1950, 15, 342–351.

17. ——. Informal factors in career achievement. *The American Journal of Sociology* 1951, 56, 407–415.

18. ——. *Men Who Manage.* New York: John Wiley & Sons, Inc., 1959.

19. Day, Robert C. and Hamblin, Robert L. Some effects of close and punitive styles of supervision. *The American Journal of Sociology* 1964, 69, 499–510.

20. Entwisle, Doris R. and Walton, John. Observations on the span of control. *Administrative Science Quarterly* 1961, 5, 522–533.

21. Fleishman, Edwin A. The measurement of leadership attitudes in industry. *Journal of Applied Psychology* 1953, 37, 153–158.

22. —— and Harris, Edwin F. Patterns of leadership behavior related to employee grievances and turnover. *Personnel Psychology* 1962, 15, 43–56.

23. —— and Peters, David R. Interpersonal values, leadership attitudes, and managerial "success." *Personnel Psychology* 1962, 15, 127–143.

24. ——; Harris, Edwin F. and Burtt, H. E. *Leadership and Supervision in Industry.* Columbus, Ohio: Bureau of Educational Research, Ohio State University, 1955.

25. Foa, Uriel G. Some correlates of the empathy of the workers with the foreman. *Journal of Applied Psychology* 1960, 44, 6–10.

26. Gaiennie, L. R. Organization control in business. *Journal of Applied Psychology* 1954, 38, 289–292.

27. Gaudet, Frederick J. and Carli, A. Ralph. Why executives fail. *Personnel Psychology,* 1957, 10, 7–21.

28. Ghiselli, Edwin E. Individuality as a factor in the success of management personnel. *Personnel Psychology* 1960, 13, 1–10.

29. ——. Maturity of self-perception in relation to managerial success. *Personnel Psychology* 1964, 17, 41–48.

30. ——. Occupational level measured through self-perception. *Personnel Psychology* 1956, 9, 169–176.

31. ——. Traits differentiating management personnel. *Personnel Psychology* 1959, 12, 534–544.

32. —— and Barthol, R. Role perceptions of successful and unsuccessful supervisors. *Journal of Applied Psychology* 1956, 40, 241–244.

33. Goodacre, Daniel M. Stimulating improved man management. *Personnel Psychology* 1963, 16, 133–143.

34. Guest, Robert H. Of time and the foreman. *Personnel,* 1956, 32, 478–486.

35. Guilford, Joan S. Temperament traits of executives and supervisors measured by the Guilford personality inventories. *Journal of Applied Psychology* 1952, 36, 228–233.

36. Haire, Mason. Biological models and empirical histories of the growth of organizations. In *Modern Organizational Theory,* Mason Haire (ed.). New York: John Wiley & Sons, Inc., 1959.

37. Halpern, Richard S. Employee unionization and foremen's attitudes. *Administrative Science Quarterly* 1961, 6, 73–88.

38. Halpin, Andrew W. The leadership ideology of aircraft commanders. *Journal of Applied Psychology* 1955, 39, 82–84.

39. Healey, James H. Coordination and control of executive functions. *Personnel* 1956, 33, 106-117.

40. Henry, W. E. The business executive: the psychodynamics of a social role. *The American Journal of Sociology* 1949, 54, 286–291.

41. Hetzler, Stanley A. Variations in role-playing patterns among different echelons of bureaucratic leaders. *American Sociological Review* 1955, 20, 700–706.

42. Indik, Bernard P; Georgopoulos, Basil S. and Seashore, Stanley E. Superior-subordinate relationships and performance. *Personnel Psychology* 1961, 14, 357–374.

43. Kahn, Robert L. and Katz, Daniel. Leadership practices in relation to productivity and morale. In *Group Dynamics,* Dorwin Cartwright and Alvin Zander (eds.). Evanston, Ill.: Row, Peterson & Company, 1960.

44. Katz, Daniel; Maccoby, Nathan and Morse, Nancy C. *Productivity, Supervision, and Morale in an Office Situation.* Ann Arbor: University of Michigan Press, 1950.

45. Kipnis, David and Lane, William P. Self-confidence and leadership. *Journal of Applied Psychology* 1962, 46, 291–295.

46. Kunnath, Jerome G. and Kerr, Willard A. Function analysis of 32 American corporate boards. *Journal of Applied Psychology* 1953, 37, 65-68.

47. Lawshe, C. H. and Nagle, Bryant F. Productivity and attitude toward supervision. *Journal of Applied Psychology* 1953, 37, 159–162.

48. Likert, Rensis. Effective supervision: an adaptive and relative process. *Personnel Psychology* 1958, 11, 317–332.

49. Maier, Norman R. F.; Hoffman, L. Richard and Read, William H. Superior-subordinate communication: the relative effectiveness of managers who held their subordinates' positions. *Personnel Psychology* 1963, 16, 1–11.

50. Marcus, Philip M. Supervision and group process. *Human Organization* 1961, 20, No. 1, 15–19.

51. Mechanic, David. Sources of power of lower participants in complex organizations. *Administrative Science Quarterly* 1962, 7, 349–364.

52. Merenda, Peter F. and Clarke, Walter V. AVA as a predictor of occupational hierarchy. *Journal of Applied Psychology* 1958, 42, 289–292.

53. Meyer, Henry D. and Pressel, Glenn L. Personality test scores in the management hierarchy. *Journal of Applied Psychology* 1954, 38, 73–80.

54. Meyer, Herbert H. A comparison of foreman and general foreman conceptions of the foreman's job responsibilities. *Personnel Psychology* 1959, 12, 445–452.

55. Miner, John B. and Culver, John E. Some aspects of the executive personality. *Journal of Applied Psychology* 1955, 39, 348–353.

56. Moore, John V. and Smith, Robert G., Jr. Some aspects of noncommissioned officer leadership. *Personnel Psychology*, 1953, 6, 427–443.

57. Nagle, Bryant F. Productivity, employee attitude and supervisor sensitivity. *Personnel Psychology* 1954, 7, 219–233.

58. Oaklander, Harold and Fleishman, Edwin A. Patterns of leadership related to organizational stress in hospital settings. *Administrative Science Quarterly* 1964, 8, 520–532.

59. Obrochta, Richard J. Foreman-worker attitude patterns. *Journal of Applied Psychology* 1960, 44, 88–91.

60. Parker, Treadway C. Relationships among measures of supervisory behavior, group behavior and situational characteristics. *Personnel Psychology* 1963, 16, 319–334.

61. Patchen, Martin. Supervisory methods and group performance norms. *Administrative Science Quarterly* 1962, 7, 275–293.

62. Patton, Wendell M., Jr. Studies in industrial empathy: III, A study of supervisory empathy in the textile industry. *Journal of Applied Psychology* 1954, 38, 285–288.

63. Pelz, Donald C. Some social factors related to performance in a research organization. *Administrative Science Quarterly* 1956, 1, 310–325.

64. Peres, Sherwood H. Performance dimensions of supervisory positions. *Personnel Psychology* 1962, 15, 405–410.

65. Porter, Lyman W. Differential self-perceptions of management personnel and line workers. *Journal of Applied Psychology* 1958, 42, 105–108.

66. Prien, Erich P. Development of a supervisor position description questionnaire. *Journal of Applied Psychology* 1963, 47, 10–14.

67. Roach, Darrell E. Factor analysis of rated supervisory behavior. *Personnel Psychology* 1956, 9, 487–498.

68. Rosen, Hjalmar. Managerial role interaction: a study of three managerial levels. *Journal of Applied Psychology* 1961, 45, 30–34.

69. Smith, Clagett G. and Ari, Oguz N. Organizational control structure and member consensus. *The American Journal of Sociology* 1964, 69, 623–638.

70. Stanton, Erwin S. Company policies and supervisors' attitudes toward supervision. *Journal of Applied Psychology* 1960, 44, 22–26.

71. Stogdill, Ralph M.; Goode, Omar S. and Day, David R. The leader behavior of corporation presidents. *Personnel Psychology* 1963, 16, 127–132.

72. ——; Shartle, Carroll L.; Wherry, Robert J. and Jaynes, William E. A factorial study of administrative behavior. *Personnel Psychology* 1955, 8, 165–180.

73. Suojanen, Waino W. The span of control—fact or fable? *Advanced Management* 1955, 20, No. 11, 5–13.

74. Tannenbaum, Arnold S. and Kahn, Robert L. Organizational control structure. *Human Relations* 1957, 10, 127–140.

75. Turner, Arthur N. Foreman, job, and company. *Human Relations* 1957, 10, 99–112.

76. ——. Interaction and sentiment in the foreman-worker relationship. *Human Organization* 1955, 14, No. 1, 10–16.

77. Whisler, Thomas L. The "assistant-to" in four administrative settings. *Administrative Science Quarterly* 1960, 5, 181–216.

78. Wilson, Robert C.; Beem, Helen P. and Comrey, Andrew L. Factors influencing organizational effectiveness. III. A survey of skilled tradesmen. *Personnel Psychology* 1953, 6, 313–325.

79. Zaleznik, Abraham. Managerial behavior and interpersonal competence. *Behavioral Science* 1964, 9, 156–166.

Index